Atlas of Sustainable Development Goals

2017 From World Development Indicators

WORLD BANK GROUP

Foreword

Reaching the targets and overcoming the challenges facing the Sustainable Development Goals requires a sharper focus on better financing, better data, and better methods of delivery, working together with partners. And immediate action is necessary if we truly want to build a world that is more just, prosperous, and secure.

The World Bank Group aims to end extreme poverty in a generation and to promote shared prosperity. It will help nations meet their national goals, and address long-term global problems such as climate change, fragility, pandemics, and stunting. The Bank's global practices and cross-cutting solution areas, broadly aligned with the SDGs, have deep knowledge and experience in virtually every cross-sectoral area.

That expertise is reflected in this *SDG Atlas*, which presents a visual and engaging guide to the challenges of the SDGs, to help policy makers, managers, and the public alike better understand them. The *Atlas* helps quantify progress, highlight some of the key issues, and identify the gaps that still remain.

The *Atlas* draws on *World Development Indicators*, a database of over 1,400 indicators for more than 220 economies, many going back more than 50 years. And it relies on the work of national and international statistical agencies around the world. I would like to acknowledge and commend them all: they play a crucial role in measuring and quantifying the development process, so that we can all make better decisions about our lives and the scarce resources we all manage.

Mahmoud Mohieldin
Senior Vice President
World Bank Group

Acknowledgments

The *Atlas of Sustainable Development Goals 2017* was produced by the Development Economics Data Group of the World Bank, in collaboration with the Global Practices and Cross-Cutting Solution Areas of the World Bank and the Office of the Senior Vice President for the 2030 Development Agenda, United Nations Relations, and Partnerships.

The publication was prepared by a team led by Umar Serajuddin, under the management of Neil Fantom and the overall direction of Haishan Fu. The editorial team was coordinated by Elizabeth Purdie and comprised Ana Florina Pirlea, Tariq Khokhar, Jomo Tariku, and Andrew Whitby. Hiroko Maeda and Andrew Whitby managed the development of the Sustainable Development Goals Interactive Dashboard.

Contributions were received from Husein Abdul-Hamid, Paola Agostini, Luis Alberto Andres, Michelle Ashwin Mehta, Raka Banerjee, Randall Brummett, Shun Chonabayashi, Davida Connon, Simon Davies, Bénédicte de la Brière, Klaus Deninger, Mustafa Dinc, Angela Elzir, Mahyar Eshragh-Tabary, Juan Feng, Caron Grown, Lewis Hawke, Timothy Herzog, Barbro Hexeberg, Thea Hilhorst, Masako Hiraga, Patrick Hoang-Vu Eozenou, Maddalena Honarati, Aira Maria Htenas, Atsushi Iimi, Sara Johansson de Silva, Bala Bhaskar Naidu Kalimili, Haruna Kashiwase, Buyant Khaltarkhuu, Silvia Kirova, Irinia I. Klytchnikova, Craig Kullmann, Samuel Lantei Mills, Shiqing Li, Libbet Loughnan, Hiroko Maeda, Eliana Carolina Rubiano Matulevich, Alejandro Moreno, Ines Zabalbeitia Mugica, Silvia Muzi, Esther Naikal, Oya Pinar Ardic Alper, Sonia Plaza, Malvina Pollock, William Prince, Anne Marie Provo, Holy Tiana Rame, Jorge Rodriguez Meza, Evis Rucaj, Fernanda Ruiz Nunez, Christopher Sall, Valentina Saltane, Maria Laura Sanchez Puerta, Meera Shekar, Avjeet Singh, Adam Stone Diehl, Victoria Strokova, Rubena Sukaj, Emi Suzuki, Robert Townsend, Tea Trumbic, Hiroki Uematsu, Michael Vaislic, Zichao Wei, Dereje Wolde, Tamirat Yacob, Junhe Yang, Soonhwa Yi, Nobuo Yoshida, Yucheng Zheng, and Urska Zrinski.

Guidance from the Office of the Senior Vice President for the 2030 Development Agenda, United Nations Relations, and Partnerships, particularly Marco Scuriatti, Mariana Dahan, Mike Kelleher and Farida Aboulmagd, and discussions with Chiyo Kanda, Nazmul Chaudhury, Andres Londono, and Sara Okada of the Operations Strategy, Results, and Risk Unit are gratefully acknowledged. The report benefited from comments and suggestions from David Rosenblatt, Tatiana Didier Brandao, Tito Cordella, Poonam Gupta, and Claudia Paz Sepulveda of the Development Economics Operations and Strategy Unit. Marianne Fay, Carter Brandon, Vivien Foster, and Melissa Johns provided invaluable advice.

Bruno Bonansea provided guidance on maps. Aziz Gokdemir, Jewel McFadden, and Nora Ridolfi oversaw printing and distribution. A team at Communications Development Incorporated—led by Bruce Ross-Larson and including Joe Caponio, Chris Trott, Lawrence Whiteley, and Elaine Wilson—managed the design, editing, and typesetting. Elysee Kiti, Lisa Burke, Juderica Diaz, and Colleen Burke provided administrative support.

About the data

The maps, charts, and analyses in this *Atlas of Sustainable Development Goals 2017* are intended to present data trends and comparisons in an accessible and visually appealing way. Given the breadth and scope of the Sustainable Development Goals (SDGs), the editors have been selective, emphasizing issues considered key by experts in the World Bank's Global Practices and Cross-Cutting Solution Areas.

The data draw on the *World Development Indicators (WDI)* database—the World Bank's compilation of internationally comparable statistics about global development and the quality of people's lives. For each of the 17 SDGs, relevant indicators have been chosen to illustrate important trends and challenges, and highlight measurement issues.

New indicators have been added to the WDI database to better reflect coverage of specific goals and targets. In some cases—for example, where country or temporal coverage is limited—supplementary data from other databases or published studies have been used. But for some targets, there may be no reliable data to use for comparisons between countries or to measure progress.

The primary international source of the data is provided in footnotes. Where indicators are available in the WDI database, the codes used to identify these indicators are given. This "CETS" code (the Catalog of Economic Time Series classification) can be used to quickly access each indicator and its metadata, using the format http://data.worldbank.org/indicator/<CETS>.

The *2017 Atlas* uses two primary methods for classifying and aggregating countries and economies — by income (as defined for the World Bank's 2017 fiscal year) and by region. These are presented in the maps on pages vi to ix.

For more information, including details on the structure of the coding scheme, the methodology, concepts and definitions, coverage, periodicity, development relevance of all WDI indicators, and the methods used for classifying countries for analytical purposes, please refer to http://datahelpdesk.worldbank.org.

The cutoff date for data is January 31, 2017.

Introduction

Between 1990 and 2013 nearly one billion people were raised out of extreme poverty. Its elimination is now a realistic prospect, although this will require both sustained growth and reduced inequality. Even then, gender inequalities continue to hold back human potential.

Undernourishment and stunting have been nearly halved since 1990, despite increasing food loss, while the burden of infectious disease has also declined. Access to water has expanded, but progress on sanitation has been slower. For too many people, access to healthcare and education still depends on personal financial means.

To date the environmental cost of growth has been high. Accumulated damage to oceanic and terrestrial ecosystems is considerable. But hopeful signs exist: while greenhouse gas emissions are at record levels, so too is renewable energy capacity.

Physical infrastructure continues to expand, but so too does population, so that urban housing and rural access to roads remain challenges, particularly in Sub-Saharan Africa.

Meanwhile the institutional infrastructure of development strengthens, with more reliable government budgeting and foreign direct investment recovering from the financial crisis. Official development assistance, however, continues to fall short of target levels.

Contents

The world by income, FY2017

Classified according to World Bank estimates of 2015 GNI per capita (current US dollar, *Atlas* method)

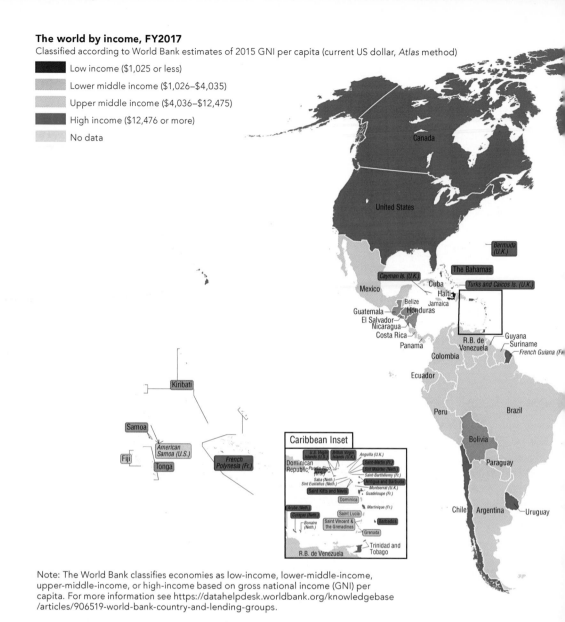

- Low income ($1,025 or less)
- Lower middle income ($1,026–$4,035)
- Upper middle income ($4,036–$12,475)
- High income ($12,476 or more)
- No data

Note: The World Bank classifies economies as low-income, lower-middle-income, upper-middle-income, or high-income based on gross national income (GNI) per capita. For more information see https://datahelpdesk.worldbank.org/knowledgebase /articles/906519-world-bank-country-and-lending-groups.

East Asia and Pacific

American Samoa	Upper middle income
Australia	High income
Brunei Darussalam	High income
Cambodia	Lower middle income
China	Upper middle income
Fiji	Upper middle income
French Polynesia	High income
Guam	High income
Hong Kong SAR, China	High income
Indonesia	Lower middle income
Japan	High income
Kiribati	Lower middle income
Korea, Dem. People's Rep.	Low income
Korea, Rep.	High income
Lao PDR	Lower middle income
Macao SAR, China	High income
Malaysia	Upper middle income
Marshall Islands	Upper middle income
Micronesia, Fed. Sts.	Lower middle income
Mongolia	Lower middle income
Myanmar	Lower middle income
Nauru	High income
New Caledonia	High income
New Zealand	High income
Northern Mariana Islands	High income
Palau	Upper middle income
Papua New Guinea	Lower middle income
Philippines	Lower middle income
Samoa	Lower middle income
Singapore	High income
Solomon Islands	Lower middle income
Thailand	Upper middle income
Timor-Leste	Lower middle income
Tonga	Lower middle income
Tuvalu	Upper middle income
Vanuatu	Lower middle income
Vietnam	Lower middle income

Europe and Central Asia

Albania	Upper middle income
Andorra	High income
Armenia	Lower middle income
Austria	High income
Azerbaijan	Upper middle income
Belarus	Upper middle income
Belgium	High income
Bosnia and Herzegovina	Upper middle income
Bulgaria	Upper middle income
Channel Islands	High income
Croatia	High income
Cyprus	High income
Czech Republic	High income
Denmark	High income
Estonia	High income
Faroe Islands	High income
Finland	High income
France	High income

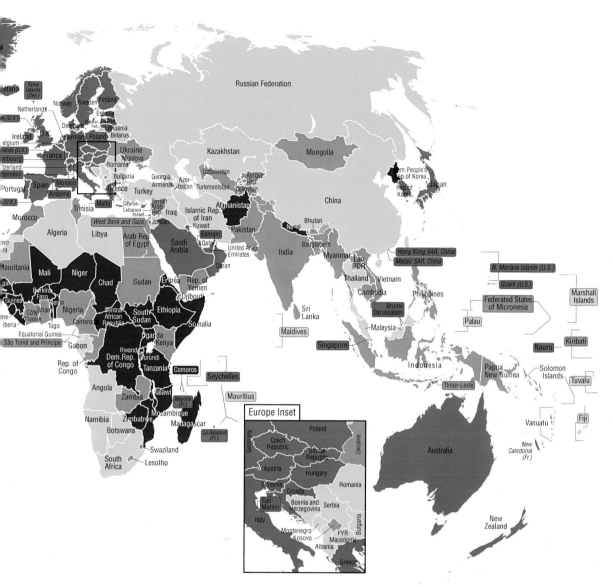

Georgia	Upper middle income	**Montenegro**	Upper middle income	**Latin America and the Caribbean**	
Germany	High income	**Netherlands**	High income	**Antigua and Barbuda**	High income
Gibraltar	High income	**Norway**	High income	**Argentina**	Upper middle income
Greece	High income	**Poland**	High income	**Aruba**	High income
Greenland	High income	**Portugal**	High income	**Bahamas, The**	High income
Hungary	High income	**Romania**	Upper middle income	**Barbados**	High income
Iceland	High income	**Russian Federation**	Upper middle income	**Belize**	Upper middle income
Ireland	High income	**San Marino**	High income	**Bolivia**	Lower middle income
Isle of Man	High income	**Serbia**	Upper middle income	**Brazil**	Upper middle income
Italy	High income	**Slovak Republic**	High income	**British Virgin Islands**	High income
Kazakhstan	Upper middle income	**Slovenia**	High income	**Cayman Islands**	High income
Kosovo	Lower middle income	**Spain**	High income	**Chile**	High income
Kyrgyz Republic	Lower middle income	**Sweden**	High income	**Colombia**	Upper middle income
Latvia	High income	**Switzerland**	High income	**Costa Rica**	Upper middle income
Liechtenstein	High income	**Tajikistan**	Lower middle income	**Cuba**	Upper middle income
Lithuania	High income	**Turkey**	Upper middle income	**Curaçao**	High income
Luxembourg	High income	**Turkmenistan**	Upper middle income	**Dominica**	Upper middle income
Macedonia, FYR	Upper middle income	**Ukraine**	Lower middle income	**Dominican Republic**	Upper middle income
Moldova	Lower middle income	**United Kingdom**	High income	**Ecuador**	Upper middle income
Monaco	High income	**Uzbekistan**	Lower middle income	**El Salvador**	Lower middle income

The world by region

Classified according to World Bank analytical grouping

- East Asia and Pacific
- Europe and Central Asia
- Latin America and Caribbean
- Middle East and North Africa
- North America
- South Asia
- Sub-Saharan Africa

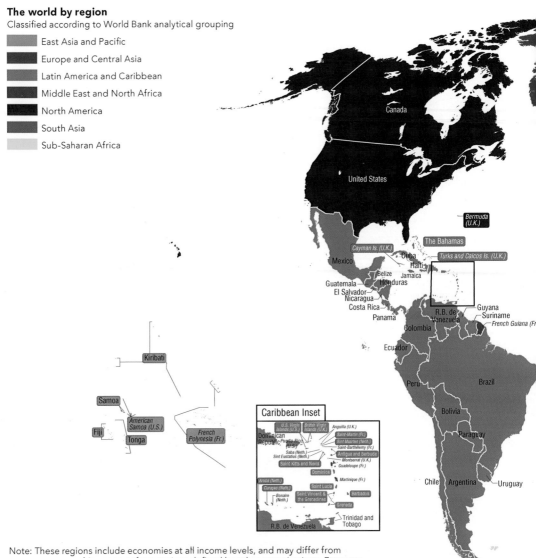

Caribbean Inset

Note: These regions include economies at all income levels, and may differ from common geographic usage or from regions defined by other organizations. For more information see https://datahelpdesk.worldbank.org/knowledgebase/articles/906519-world-bank-country-and-lending-groups.

Grenada	Upper middle income	**Trinidad and Tobago**	High income	**Malta**	High income
Guatemala	Lower middle income	**Turks and Caicos**		**Morocco**	Lower middle income
Guyana	Upper middle income	Islands	High income	**Oman**	High income
Haiti	Low income	Uruguay	High income	**Qatar**	High income
Honduras	Lower middle income	Venezuela, RB	Upper middle income	**Saudi Arabia**	High income
Jamaica	Upper middle income	Virgin Islands (U.S.)	High income	**Syrian Arab Republic**	Lower middle income
Mexico	Upper middle income			**Tunisia**	Lower middle income
Nicaragua	Lower middle income	**Middle East and North Africa**		**United Arab Emirates**	High income
Panama	Upper middle income	Algeria	Upper middle income	**West Bank and Gaza**	Lower middle income
Paraguay	Upper middle income	Bahrain	High income	**Yemen, Rep.**	Lower middle income
Peru	Upper middle income	Djibouti	Lower middle income		
Puerto Rico	High income	Egypt, Arab Rep.	Lower middle income	**North America**	
Sint Maarten	High income	Iran, Islamic Rep.	Upper middle income	**Bermuda**	High income
St. Kitts and Nevis	High income	Iraq	Upper middle income	**Canada**	High income
St. Lucia	Upper middle income	Israel	High income	**United States**	High income
St. Martin	High income	Jordan	Upper middle income		
St. Vincent and		Kuwait	High income	**South Asia**	
the Grenadines	Upper middle income	Lebanon	Upper middle income	**Afghanistan**	Low income
Suriname	Upper middle income	Libya	Upper middle income	**Bangladesh**	Lower middle income

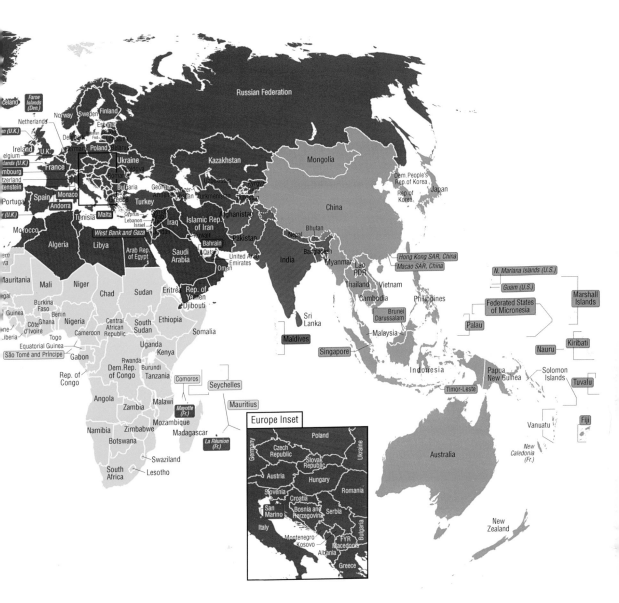

Bhutan	Lower middle income
India	Lower middle income
Maldives	Upper middle income
Nepal	Low income
Pakistan	Lower middle income
Sri Lanka	Lower middle income

Sub-Saharan Africa

Angola	Upper middle income
Benin	Low income
Botswana	Upper middle income
Burkina Faso	Low income
Burundi	Low income
Cabo Verde	Lower middle income
Cameroon	Lower middle income
Central African Republic	Low income
Chad	Low income
Comoros	Low income

Congo, Dem. Rep.	Low income
Congo, Rep.	Lower middle income
Côte d'Ivoire	Lower middle income
Equatorial Guinea	Upper middle income
Eritrea	Low income
Ethiopia	Low income
Gabon	Upper middle income
Gambia, The	Low income
Ghana	Lower middle income
Guinea	Low income
Guinea-Bissau	Low income
Kenya	Lower middle income
Lesotho	Lower middle income
Liberia	Low income
Madagascar	Low income
Malawi	Low income
Mali	Low income
Mauritania	Lower middle income
Mauritius	Upper middle income

Mozambique	Low income
Namibia	Upper middle income
Niger	Low income
Nigeria	Lower middle income
Rwanda	Low income
São Tomé and Principe	Lower middle income
Senegal	Low income
Seychelles	High income
Sierra Leone	Low income
Somalia	Low income
South Africa	Upper middle income
South Sudan	Low income
Sudan	Lower middle income
Swaziland	Lower middle income
Tanzania	Low income
Togo	Low income
Uganda	Low income
Zambia	Lower middle income
Zimbabwe	Low income

🚶‍♀️ No poverty

1

End poverty in all its forms everywhere

An estimated 766 million people, or 10.7 percent of the world's population, lived in extreme poverty in 2013. In 2012 the extreme poverty rate stood at 12.4 percent globally, and over the year the number of people living below the international poverty line of $1.90 a day fell by 114 million. Goal 1 aims to end poverty in all its forms by 2030. It also seeks to ensure social protection for poor and vulnerable people, to increase access to basic services, and to support those harmed by conflict and climate-related disasters.

Eradicating extreme poverty

Of the world's population, 35 percent—1.8 billion—lived in extreme poverty in 1990. Half were in East Asia and Pacific, where the extreme poverty rate was 60 percent, making it the poorest region at that time (figure 1a). While all regions have made progress, the most significant was in East Asia and Pacific, which recorded an extreme poverty rate of just 3.5 percent in 2013, a dramatic fall driven largely by China. In South Asia extreme poverty also fell sharply, to a third of its 1990 level (from 45 percent to 15 percent). Even with substantial progress, considerable challenges remain: despite a decline in the extreme poverty rate in Sub-Saharan Africa, to 41 percent, the region's population growth means that 389 million people lived on less than $1.90 a day in 2013, 113 million more than in 1990.

Sub-Saharan Africa now accounts for half the world's extreme poor (figure 1b).

Reducing poverty in all its dimensions according to national definitions

The target of eliminating extreme poverty by 2030 uses a globally comparable poverty line as a benchmark. Goal 1 also looks to halve the share of the population living in poverty as defined by national authorities (target 1.2). National poverty lines typically reflect a threshold below which a person's minimum nutrition, clothing, and shelter needs cannot be met, consistent with the country's economic and social circumstances. So, richer countries tend to have higher poverty lines than poorer ones (figure 1c), and in some cases a richer country may have a higher national poverty rate than a poorer country.

1a The extreme poverty rate and the number of people living in extreme poverty have fallen in almost every region
Number and share of population living on less than $1.90 a day (2011 purchasing power parity or PPP) (%), 1990 and 2013

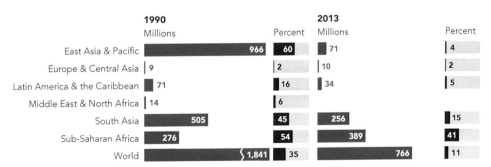

Note: For this indicator, regional aggregates exclude certain high income countries (World Bank Group. Poverty and Shared Prosperity 2016: Taking on Inequality. Washington, DC: World Bank., p. 49). 2013 estimates for Middle East and North Africa are not shown because survey coverage is too low.
Source: World Bank PovcalNet (http://iresearch.worldbank.org/PovcalNet/); WDI (SI.POV.DDAY).

1b The number of people living in extreme poverty has fallen in most countries but has risen in many Sub-Saharan African countries

People living on less than $1.90 a day (2011 PPP), 1990 and 2013

1990

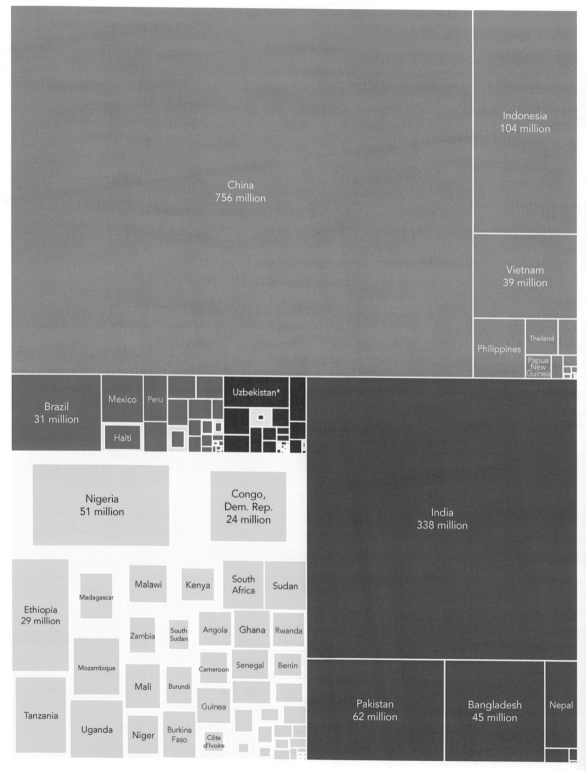

*Uzbekistan (1990) based on 1998 rate because of quality issues with earlier survey data.

2013

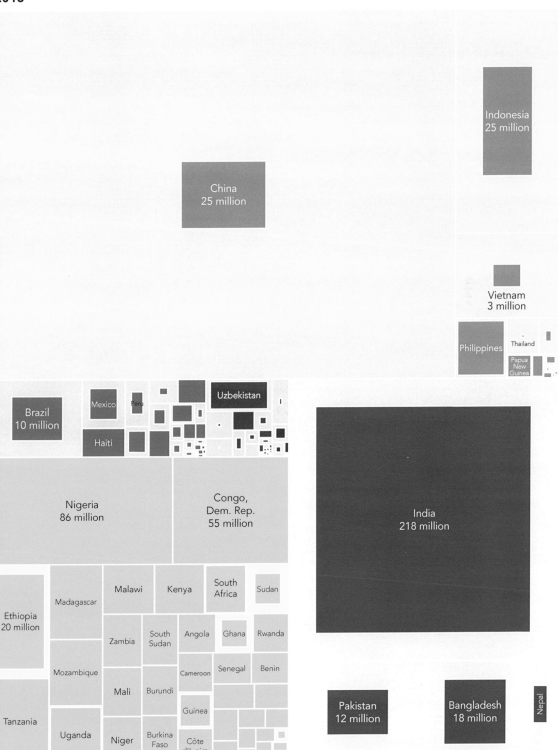

Indonesia 25 million

China 25 million

Vietnam 3 million

Philippines

Thailand

Papua New Guinea

Brazil 10 million

Mexico

Peru

Uzbekistan

Haiti

Nigeria 86 million

Congo, Dem. Rep. 55 million

India 218 million

Ethiopia 20 million

Madagascar

Malawi

Kenya

South Africa

Sudan

Zambia

South Sudan

Angola

Ghana

Rwanda

Mozambique

Cameroon

Senegal

Benin

Mali

Burundi

Tanzania

Guinea

Uganda

Niger

Burkina Faso

Côte d'Ivoire

Pakistan 12 million

Bangladesh 18 million

Nepal

Source: World Bank PovcalNet; WDI (SI.POV.DDAY).

1c Richer countries tend to have higher national poverty lines

National per capita per day poverty line, 2000–12 (2011 PPP $)

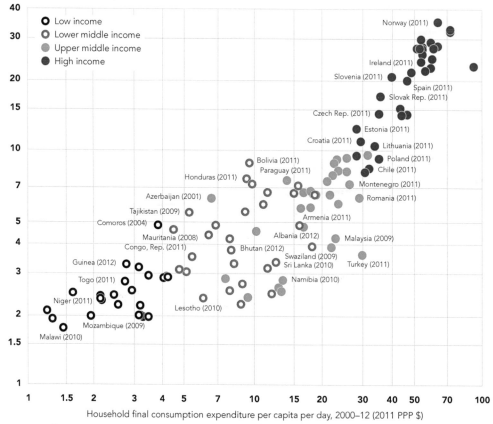

Source: Jolliffe, D. M., and E. B. Prydz. 2016, *Estimating International Poverty Lines from Comparable National Thresholds,* Policy Research Working Paper WPS 7606, Washington, DC: World Bank Group.

Countries define monetary poverty lines using either income or consumption. In the years measured up to 2013 (over 9–15 year intervals), 17 of 45 countries with data reduced their poverty rates by more than half. Another 4 countries were on track to halve their poverty in 15 years if reduction trends continued. In the remainder, poverty rate declines were smaller, and indeed the rate increased in a few countries (figure 1d).

In general, countries maintain the same national poverty lines over time, adjusting them for inflation to remain constant in real terms. But some European countries (such as the Czech Republic, Hungary, and Poland) use a relative poverty line, usually setting their thresholds at 60 percent of the country's median income or consumption. In such cases, measured poverty may not decline, even if incomes are rising, and halving poverty would be possible only by drastically reducing inequality.

Some countries—such as Bhutan, Bolivia, Colombia, Costa Rica, El Salvador, and Mexico —have adopted measures that aim to capture the multidimensional nature of poverty by assessing how households are deprived in different ways (in health, education, housing, and labor market opportunities).

1d National poverty rates have fallen substantially in many countries over the last 15 years

Reduction in poverty headcount ratio at the national poverty line (%)

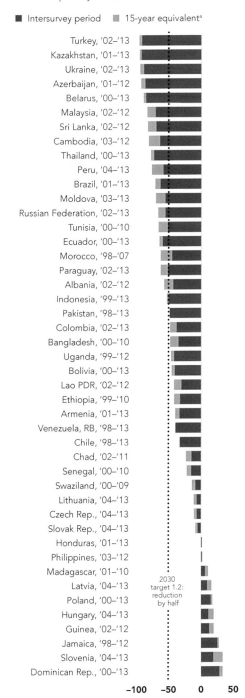

- ■ Intersurvey period
- ■ 15-year equivalent[a]

Turkey, '02–'13
Kazakhstan, '01–'13
Ukraine, '02–'13
Azerbaijan, '01–'12
Belarus, '00–'13
Malaysia, '02–'12
Sri Lanka, '02–'12
Cambodia, '03–'12
Thailand, '00–'13
Peru, '04–'13
Brazil, '01–'13
Moldova, '03–'13
Russian Federation, '02–'13
Tunisia, '00–'10
Ecuador, '00–'13
Morocco, '98–'07
Paraguay, '02–'13
Albania, '02–'12
Indonesia, '99–'13
Pakistan, '98–'13
Colombia, '02–'13
Bangladesh, '00–'10
Uganda, '99–'12
Bolivia, '00–'13
Lao PDR, '02–'12
Ethiopia, '99–'10
Armenia, '01–'13
Venezuela, RB, '98–'13
Chile, '98–'13
Chad, '02–'11
Senegal, '00–'10
Swaziland, '00–'09
Lithuania, '04–'13
Czech Rep., '04–'13
Slovak Rep., '04–'13
Honduras, '01–'13
Philippines, '03–'12
Madagascar, '01–'10
Latvia, '04–'13
Poland, '00–'13
Hungary, '04–'13
Guinea, '02–'12
Jamaica, '98–'12
Slovenia, '04–'13
Dominican Rep., '00–'13

2030 target 1.2: reduction by half

−100 −50 0 50

a. Based on average compound annual growth rate.
Source: WDI (SI.POV.NAHC).

Expanding social protection for those most in need

Social protection programs, which can increase the resilience of poor and vulnerable people and the opportunities available to them (target 1.3), are essential to ending poverty. Programs include social assistance (such as cash and in-kind transfers), social insurance (such as pensions and unemployment insurance), and active labor market programs (such as skills training and wage subsidies). They reduce poverty by ensuring adequate protection against different types of shocks; by redistributing incomes to promote a more equitable society; and by reducing perceived risk, thereby promoting the accumulation of human capital and productive investment opportunities.

Few poor people, however, are covered by social protection programs. Social assistance coverage in many low-income countries remains especially limited; in Burkina Faso and the Democratic Republic of Congo fewer than one in 10 people in the poorest quintile receives any social assistance (figure 1e). Social insurance coverage is even narrower, with fewer than one in 20 people in the poorest quintile benefiting in low-income countries. Coverage in some lower-middle-income countries is also restricted, with only a few countries, such as the Kyrgyz Republic and Ukraine, extending social insurance to half the people in the poorest quintile.

To be effective in reducing poverty, social protection benefits must reach the poor and vulnerable. But in low-income countries the opposite is true: the richest quintile receives a much higher share of social assistance benefits than the poorest quintile (figure 1f). In Rwanda the richest quintile receives around seven times more in benefits than the poorest quintile. For social assistance to be pro-poor, the poorest quintile's share of benefits needs to be higher than 20 percent.

1e Social protection coverage among the poorest quintile tends to be lower in low-income countries

Coverage of social assistance and social insurance, poorest quintile, most recent year available during 2010–14 (%)

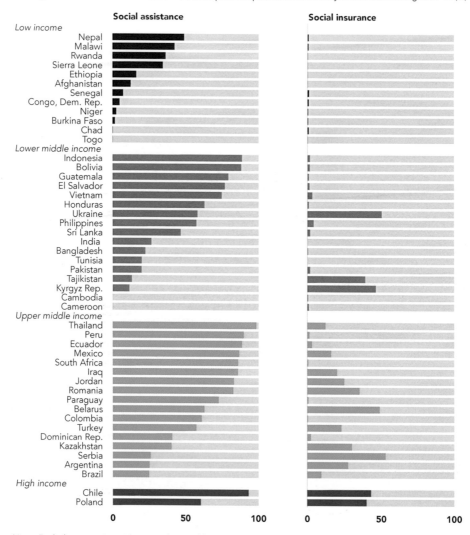

Note: Excludes countries with a population of fewer than 5 million.
Source: World Bank ASPIRE database.

Securing land rights

Tenure security is crucial for encouraging productive investment, sustainable land management, and access to finance (target 1.4). Clear land rights help reduce conflict, increase transparency, and generate revenues for public services through property taxes. Recognizing rights is vital both for indigenous communities and for women, bolstering their bargaining power, household welfare, and equality of opportunity through asset ownership.

Data on tenure security and on the mapping and registering of private plots come from administrative records of national land registries and cadasters and from census and multitopic household surveys by national statistical agencies (figure 1g).

Around 65 percent of Organisation for Economic Co-operation and Development countries register most private plots across the country. But fewer than 5 percent of countries in Latin America and the Caribbean

1f In many countries the poorest get a smaller share of social assistance benefits than the richest
Benefit incidence of social assistance and social insurance, by income quintile, most recent year available during 2010–14 (%)

■ Poorest quintile　■ Middle three quintiles　■ Richest quintile

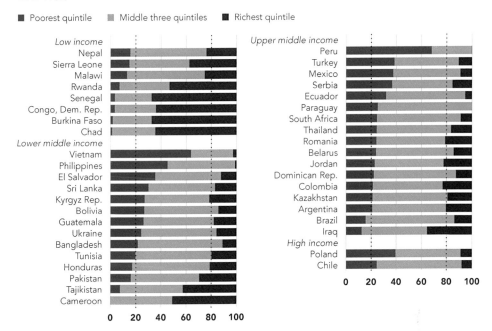

Note: Excludes countries with a population of fewer than 5 million.
Source: World Bank ASPIRE database.

1g Mapping and registering private plots countrywide are less likely in Latin America and the Caribbean and Sub-Saharan Africa
Share of countries that have the majority of private plots in the country (or main city) registered or mapped, 2016 (%)

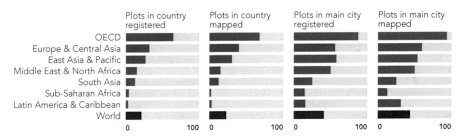

Note: Regional data exclude OECD member countries.
Source: World Bank Doing Business 2016.

and Sub-Saharan Africa do. The registration of plots in main cities is higher across all regions.

A functional land registration system tends to be strongly linked to women's rights to land and to policies supporting women's rights. Registering women's rights to land prevents these rights from being lost, through inheritance or divorce, and allows individuals to advocate for enforcing rights that are guaranteed on paper but not elsewhere.

In Rwanda, where 97 percent of households report having documented rights to land, nearly 77 percent of women in those households say they held documented rights, either individually or jointly. In Colombia just over half of households are registered, but only 11 percent of women have documented land rights.

◡ Zero hunger

2 End hunger, achieve food security and improved nutrition, and promote sustainable agriculture

Undernourishment declined globally from 19 percent to 11 percent in the past quarter century, while child stunting fell from 40 percent to 23 percent. But populations and food demand continue to grow, especially in South Asia and Sub-Saharan Africa. Ending hunger and all forms of malnutrition by 2030 requires faster downward trends. Goal 2 also addresses poverty and food insecurity through enhancing agricultural productivity and sustainability.

Ending hunger and malnutrition

An end to hunger is an end to chronic undernourishment, the state of not acquiring enough food to meet the daily minimum dietary energy requirements over a year. The prevalence of undernourishment declined by 8 percentage points between 1991 and 2015 globally, leaving 793 million people currently affected (see figure 2d on page 10).

Over a third of all undernourished people live in South Asia, while Sub-Saharan Africa and East Asia and Pacific each account for around a quarter (see figure 2c on page 10). All these regions have seen fairly steady declines in the prevalence of undernourishment since 1990. Continuing progress is not assured, however: the Middle East and North Africa has stagnated in recent years, if at the relatively low level of 8.2 percent. Ending hunger by 2030 requires accelerated efforts to achieve faster global declines (target 2.1).

Malnutrition refers to both undernutrition and overnutrition. Goal 2 aims to end "all forms of malnutrition" by 2030 (target 2.2). It encompasses the World Health Assembly (WHA) 2025 targets of a 40 percent reduction in the number of children under-five who are stunted (too short for age), no increase in childhood overweight (too heavy for height), a 50 percent reduction of anemia in women of reproductive age, and increasing the rate of exclusive breastfeeding in the first six months to at least 50 percent.

Reducing stunting

The number of stunted children has declined steadily since 1990, and many countries are on course to meet the target of reducing stunting by 2025.[1] But the absolute number of stunted children increased in Sub-Saharan Africa from nearly 45 million in 1990 to 57 million in 2015, and the region will not meet the WHA target of reducing the number by 40 percent if the current trend is not reversed (figure 2a). Moreover, the East Asia and Pacific downward trend is driven largely by reductions in China; Indonesia and the Philippines require accelerated progress to reach the 2025 target.

Aggregate trends mask inequalities in child malnutrition among the rich and the poor. Evidence from 80 countries from 1990 to 2011 shows persistent inequalities in child undernutrition, particularly stunting, with countries showing little or no progress toward bridging the gap between the wealthy and the poor.[2]

Among 10 countries with the highest child stunting prevalence in 2010–15, many exhibit a wide gap between the poorest and the richest quintile of the population (figure 2b). This gap is the widest in three lower-middle-income countries, Lao PDR (a gap of 41 percentage points), Pakistan (39), and Yemen (33). The gap in other high-prevalence countries ranges from 12 percentage points (Benin) to 29 (Burundi). Cameroon, Nepal, Nigeria, and Peru also have wide gaps in child stunting prevalence by wealth quintile, though their average prevalences are not as high.

2a Child stunting is steadily declining in most regions but increasing in Sub-Saharan Africa
Number of children under age 5 that are stunted, height for age (millions)

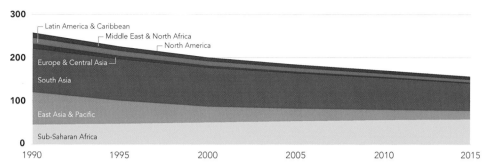

Source: United Nations Children's Fund, World Health Organization, and World Bank, 2016, *Levels and Trends in Child Malnutrition*, New York; WDI (SH.STA.STNT.ZS).

2b Child stunting can vary as much within countries as between countries
Share of children under 5 that are stunted, height for age (%)

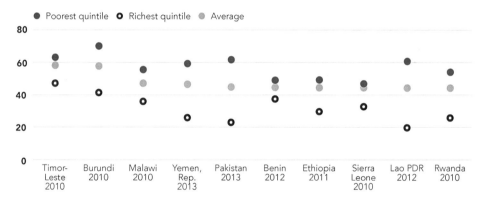

Source: World Bank Health, Nutrition, and Population Statistics database (SH.STA.STNT.Q1.ZS, SH.STA.STNT.Q5.ZS, SH.STA.STNT.QT.ZS).

Enhancing agricultural productivity and food security

The prevalence of undernourishment provides only a partial picture of the food security situation. To contribute to a more comprehensive assessment of the multiple dimensions and manifestations of food insecurity and to better inform policy responses, the Food and Agriculture Organization has compiled a preliminary set of food security indicators, available for most countries and years. One such indicator is the depth of food deficit, measured as the amount of calories needed to lift the undernourished from their current status, everything else being constant.

The depth of food deficit has declined the fastest in East Asia and Pacific and Latin America and the Caribbean, but persists at relatively high levels in Sub-Saharan Africa and South Asia. Globally, the depth of food deficit is about half of what it was 20 years ago (figure 2e). Continuing population growth and rising food demand coupled with the projected negative impacts of climate change on agriculture in the most vulnerable countries add to the challenge of sustaining and accelerating progress across all regions.[3]

The populations of both Sub-Saharan Africa and South Asia are increasing faster than elsewhere (figure 2f). Projected rises in those two regions over the next 15 years will together

2c Undernourishment is most widespread in Sub-Saharan Africa, South Asia, and East Asia and Pacific

Prevalence of undernourishment, 2015 (% of population)

- 0–5
- 5–10
- 10–20
- 20–40
- Over 40
- No data

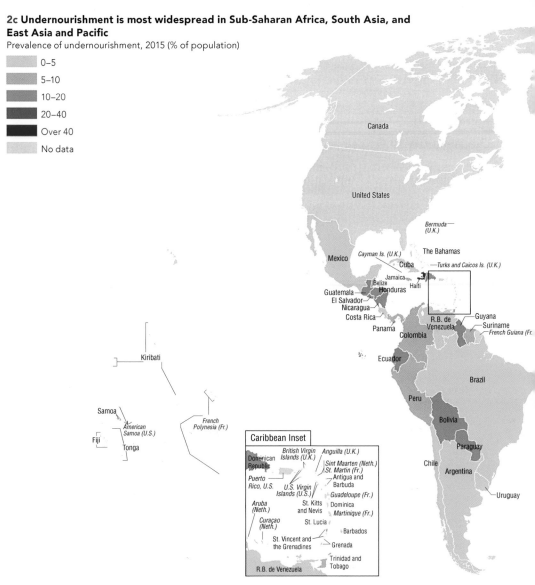

Source: Food and Agriculture Organization; WDI (SN.ITK.DEFC.ZS).

2d Undernourishment, declining in almost every region, remains highest in Sub-Saharan Africa and South Asia

Prevalence of undernourishment (% of population)

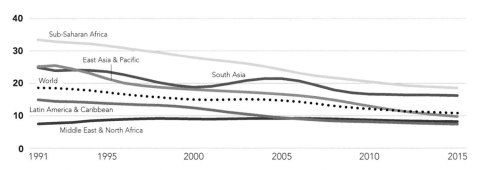

Note: Data refer to the middle year of three-year intervals. For example, data for 2005 are estimates for 2004–06. Data are not available for Europe and Central Asia or North America.
Source: Food and Agriculture Organization; WDI (SN.ITK.DEFC.ZS).

2e The depth of food deficit across regions has narrowed but is still highest in Sub-Saharan Africa and South Asia

Depth of food deficit (kilocalories per person per day)

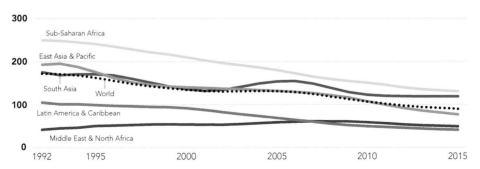

Note: Data are not available for Europe and Central Asia or North America.
Source: Food and Agriculture Organization, Food Security Statistics; WDI (SN.ITK.DFCT).

2f Two-thirds of the projected growth in the world's population by 2030 is in the high–food deficit regions of Sub-Saharan Africa and South Asia

Increase in population since 1990, projected from 2015 (millions)

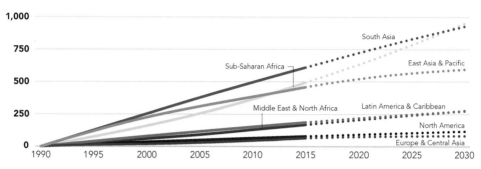

Source: World Bank Health, Nutrition, and Population Statistics: Population estimates and projections; WDI (SP.POP.TOTL).

2g Cereal yield growth rates have varied across regions, more than doubling in Sub-Saharan Africa and more than halving in the Middle East and North Africa

Cereal yield average annual growth rate (%)

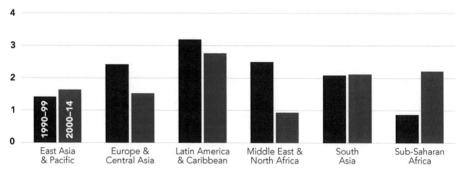

Source: Food and Agriculture Organization; WDI (AG.YLD.CREL.KG).

account for around two-thirds of the change in the global population, anticipated to rise by 16 percent over that period. At the same time, food demand is projected to rise by at least 20 percent globally, with the largest increases in Sub-Saharan Africa (55 percent) and South Asia (25 percent).

Improving agricultural performance will be central to addressing poverty and food insecurity, as more than three-quarters of poor people still live in rural areas, and nearly two-thirds of the world's poor work in agriculture.[4] Although cereal yields have accelerated in Sub-Saharan Africa since the 1990s (doubling the cereal yield growth rate), they are not rising fast enough to meet growing food demand. If projected food demand to 2030 in

Sub-Saharan Africa is to be met by productivity gains alone, cereal yields will need to increase at 3 percent a year, about a third higher than the 2.2 percent rate during 2000–14.

Some growth will be met by expanding production to areas currently not under cultivation, but growth in yields will become more important. Climate change could further reduce yields.[5] In the Middle East and North Africa, cereal yield growth has slowed from 2.5 percent annually in the 1990s to 0.9 percent in 2000–14, less than half the 2 percent annual population growth rate in the region since 2000 (figure 2g). Current cereal yields are highest in East Asia and Pacific (4.9 tons a hectare), and Latin America and the Caribbean (4.1); and lowest in Sub-Saharan Africa (1.5) and

2h The share of children who are overweight is increasing, particularly in lower-middle-income countries

Share of children under 5 who are overweight (%)

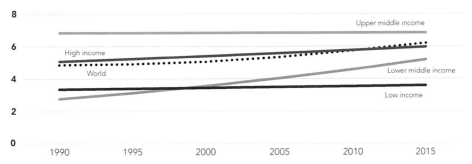

Source: World Health Organization Global Database on Child Growth and Malnutrition; WDI (SH.STA.OWGH.ZS).

the Middle East and North Africa (2.3). Yield growth, climate resilience, and enhanced trade will all be needed to help end hunger by 2030.

Addressing overweight and obesity

Overweight and obesity are rising in nearly every country, creating a major global challenge.[6] Both the prevalence and absolute number of overweight children under five are increasing globally. Upper-middle-income countries have the highest levels of overweight prevalence, while rates have been increasing most rapidly in lower-middle-income and in high-income countries. As both prevalence and population continue to rise, so will the numbers of overweight children. (figure 2h). The WHO target of no increase in childhood overweight by 2025 will not be met if current trends continue.

Notes

1. International Food Policy Research Institute. 2016. *2016 Global Food Policy Report*. Washington, DC. http://dx.doi.org/10.2499/9780896295827.

2. Bredenkamp, C., L. R. Buisman, and E. Van de Poel. 2014. "Persistent Inequalities in Child Undernutrition: Evidence from 80 Countries, from 1990 to Today." *International Journal of Epidemiology* 43(4): 1–8.

3. World Bank. 2016. *Poverty and Shared Prosperity 2016: Taking on Inequality.* Washington, DC. doi: 10.1596/978-1-4648-0958-3.

4. World Bank. 2016. *Poverty and Shared Prosperity 2016: Taking on Inequality.* Washington, DC. doi: 10.1596/978-1-4648-0958-3.

5. Townsend, Robert. 2015. Ending poverty and hunger by 2030: an agenda for the global food system. Washington, DC: World Bank Group.

6. International Food Policy Research Institute. 2016. *Global Nutrition Report 2016: From Promise to Impact: Ending Malnutrition by 2030.* Washington, DC.

—⩗❤ Good health and well-being

3 Ensure healthy lives and promote well-being for all at all ages

In 2015, 303,000 mothers died from complications in pregnancy or childbirth—216 per 100,000 live births. In Sub-Saharan Africa the rate was more than twice that. Both there and in South Asia only half of births are attended by skilled staff, and the number of newborn deaths in the first month is also high, at around 30 per 1,000 births. Goal 3 addresses these and other causes of premature death and seeks universal health coverage, so that people can obtain health care without great financial penalty.

Reducing maternal and child mortality

Fewer women and babies are dying during pregnancy, childbirth, and soon after than ever before recorded. But both Sub-Saharan Africa and South Asia have some way to go to reduce the deaths of mothers to fewer than 70 deaths per 100,000 live births (target 3.1) and neonatal mortality to fewer than 12 per 1,000 live births (target 3.2; figure 3a). In these two regions only half the births were attended by skilled health staff, far fewer than the nearly 90 percent or more elsewhere across the globe. Fewer pregnancies would reduce the number of maternal deaths, but more than 50 percent of married women in low-income countries report that their demand for family planning is not satisfied by modern contraceptive methods.

Ending the epidemics of AIDS, tuberculosis, and malaria

AIDS, tuberculosis, and malaria together affect hundreds of millions of people worldwide, and putting an end to these diseases is a priority under Goal 3 (target 3.3). While the incidence of HIV infection has been declining globally since 1995, the disease is still prevalent in Sub-Saharan Africa, where 3 of every 1,000 uninfected people ages 15–49 contracted it in 2015 (figure 3b). The number of people living with HIV, now at more than 36 million globally, continues to rise since access to antiretroviral therapy increases survival rates.[1]

The incidence of tuberculosis, also declining since the early 2000s, remains a global health challenge, especially in Sub-Saharan Africa

3a More deaths occur during birth and early childhood in regions lacking skilled health staff

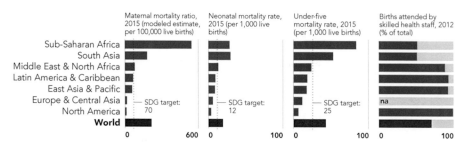

na is not available.
Source: WHO, UNICEF, UNFPA, World Bank Group, and United Nations Population Division; UN Inter-agency Group for Child Mortality Estimation; WDI (SH.STA.BRTC.ZS, SH.STA.MMRT, SH.DYN.NMRT, SH.DYN.MORT).

3b The rate of new HIV cases in Sub-Saharan Africa has declined dramatically since 1995
Incidence of HIV (% of uninfected population ages 15–49)

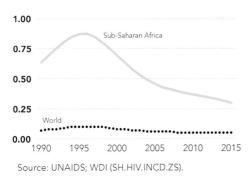

Source: UNAIDS; WDI (SH.HIV.INCD.ZS).

3c Sub-Saharan Africa still has over twice the global rate of new tuberculosis cases
Incidence of tuberculosis (per 100,000 people)

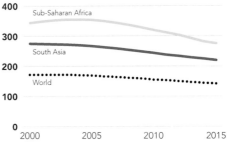

Source: WHO; WDI (SH.TBS.INCD).

(276 new cases per 100,000 people in 2015) and South Asia (220; figure 3c). Worldwide there were 10.4 million new tuberculosis cases and 1.4 million deaths due to tuberculosis in 2015.[2]

In 2015 the global incidence of malaria was about 94 per 1,000 persons at risk (figure 3d). Sub-Saharan Africa bears the highest burden, with an incidence of 234 per 1,000 persons at risk. Countries with the highest incidence include Mali (449 per 1,000 persons at risk) and Burkina Faso (389 per 1,000 persons at risk).

Tackling premature mortality from noncommunicable diseases and suicide

As the incidence of, and deaths from, communicable diseases such as malaria and tuberculosis fall, the share of deaths from noncommunicable diseases increases. Globally, premature death (before age 70) caused by the four major noncommunicable diseases —cardiovascular disease, cancer, diabetes, and chronic respiratory disease—declined 16 percent between 2000 and 2015. To reduce it by one-third by 2030 requires accelerating the current trend (target 3.4). Nine of the 12 highest national rates in 2015 were in East Asia and Pacific or Europe and Central Asia, with Papua New Guinea the highest, where the probability of 30-year-old people dying from these noncommunicable diseases before their 70th birthday is 36 percent (figure 3e).

Mental health is also a focus of target 3.4. Suicide accounts for 8.2 percent of deaths among young adults ages 15–29 globally and is the second leading cause of death after road traffic injuries for that age group.[3] Suicide rates for all ages tend to be higher in Europe and Central Asia and in high-income countries (figure 3f).

Preventing substance abuse

In 2012, 3.3 million deaths—6 percent of deaths worldwide—were attributed to alcohol consumption, predominantly through injuries or noncommunicable diseases.[4] Global consumption was 6.3 liters of pure alcohol per person ages 15 and older in 2015, equivalent to 3 liters of beer (4 percent alcohol) a week. Consumption was highest in Europe and Central Asia (10.2 liters of pure alcohol per person a year) and lowest in the Middle East and North Africa (0.8 liters; figure 3g). Goal 3 includes in its agenda preventing and treating harmful use of alcohol (target 3.5).

Extending financial protection

Universal health coverage strives for people having access to health care without suffering undue financial hardship. Achieving it would prevent people from falling into poverty due to illness and give people the opportunity to lead healthier and more productive lives (target 3.8).

3d Malaria is widespread in much of the tropics, but Sub-Saharan Africa is the worst affected
Confirmed cases of malaria, 2015 (per 1,000 at-risk people)[a]

■ No confirmed cases	■ 0.1–10	■ More than 100
■ >0–0.1	■ 10–100	■ No data

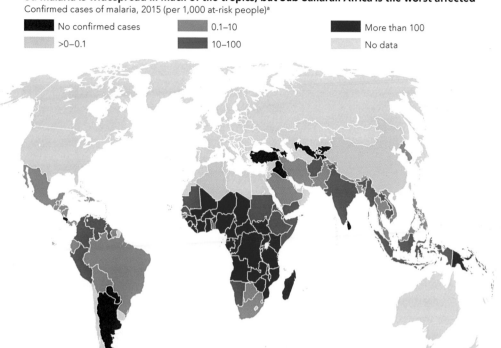

a. People living in areas of endemic malaria.
Source: WHO; WDI (SH.MLR.INCD.P3).

3e Noncommunicable diseases kill a greater proportion of middle-age people in low- and middle-income countries
Mortality from cardiovascular disease, cancer, diabetes, or chronic respiratory disease between ages 30 and 70, 2015 (%)

■ 5–15	■ 15–25	■ Over 25	■ No data

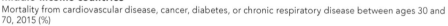
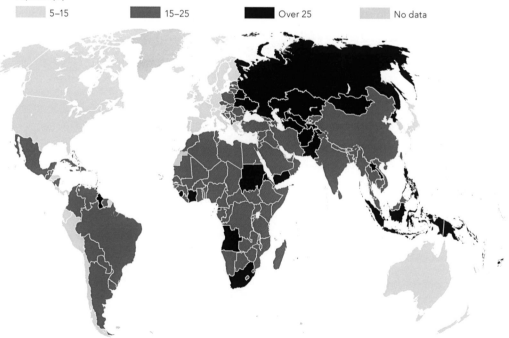

Source: WHO; WDI (SH.DYN.NCOM.ZS).

3f High suicide rates are not restricted to any one region
Suicide mortality rate, 2015 (per 100,000 people)

| | 0–6 | | 6–12 | | More than 12 | | No data |

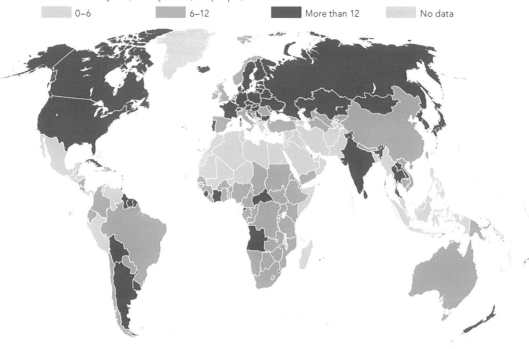

Source: WHO; WDI (SH.STA.SUIC.P5).

3g Consumption of alcohol was highest in Europe and Central Asia
Pure alcohol consumed per person ages 15 and older, projected estimates, 2015 (liters per year)

| | 0–4 | | 4–8 | | 8–12 | | More than 12 | | No data |

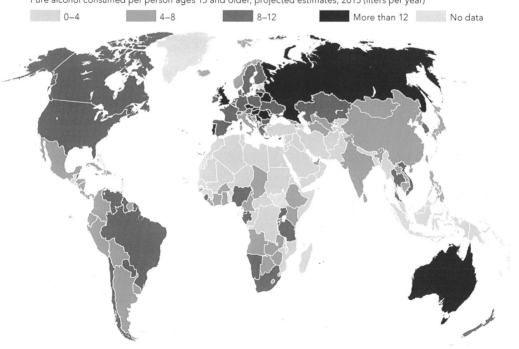

Source: WHO; WDI (SH.ALC.PCAP.LI).

3h Health financing is dominated by out-of-pocket payments in poorer countries

Out-of-pocket payments as a share of total health expenditure, 2014 (%)

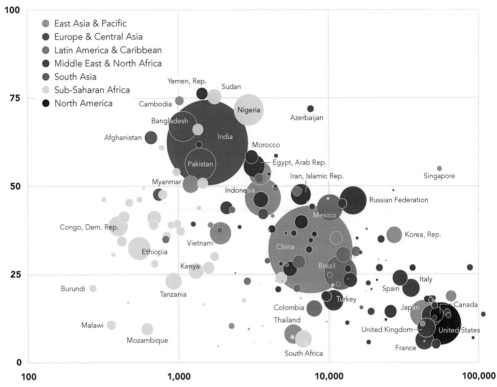

Gross national income per capita ($, *Atlas* method, log scale)

Note: Circle size is proportional to population size.
Source: WHO Global Health Expenditure database; World Bank National Accounts database; OECD National Accounts database; WDI (SH.XPD.OOPC.TO.ZS, NY.GNP.PCAP.CD).

Health care financing in many low- and middle-income countries is still dominated by high out-of-pocket expenditures (figure 3h). Weaknesses in prepayment mechanisms such as taxation or health insurance—and user fees imposed at the point of service—often impede access to care, especially for the poorest.

A meaningful measure of universal coverage needs to reflect the ability of a health system to protect people from the financial risks associated with paying for health care. Universal coverage should offer protection from catastrophic health expenditures—out-of-pocket payments representing a large share of household consumption, usually with a specific

threshold. It should also protect people from impoverishing out-of-pocket payments.

The latest available consumption survey data for 110 countries show that in the median country about 7 percent of the population face out-of-pocket payments in excess of 10 percent of their total consumption, including 3 percent for whom health payments represent 15 percent or more of their consumption.[5] Every year, 0.74 percent of people are pushed into extreme poverty (living on less than $1.90 a day) by out-of-pocket health payments, and 12 percent of those already below the $1.90 line are driven deeper into poverty. These problems prevail more in countries relying heavily on out-of-pocket payments to fund health care (figure 3i).

3i In systems reliant on out-of-pocket payments, the risk of catastrophic expenditure is higher

People experiencing expenditure beyond threshold during year (% of total population)

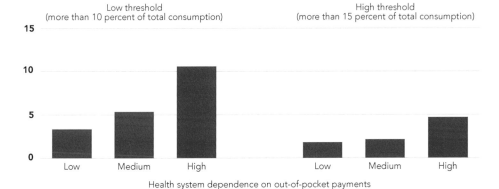

Note: Low dependence means 20% or less of national health expenditure is funded by out-of-pocket payments; medium, 20–40%; high, more than 40%. Figure shown is the median for each group. Latest available surveys for 110 countries (2000–15).
Source: WHO Global Health Expenditure database; WDI (SH.XPD.OOPC.TO.ZS); World Bank analysis of nationally representative household consumption surveys.

Filling the data gaps

Systematically collecting health data is challenging. Even a basic indicator like under-five mortality requires two complete counts, of live births and child deaths by precise age, which are not always available. More complex data, such as cause of death, require even more detailed, complete, and correctly coded information. Civil registration and vital statistics systems to record these life events remain weak in many countries. Only an estimated half or fewer deaths worldwide are registered with cause of death information. In some countries a verbal autopsy (based on interviews with friends and family members) determines the probable cause of out-of-facility deaths, but distinguishing among noncommunicable causes of death using this method remains a challenge.[6] Effective monitoring of the Goal 3 targets will require greater investment in such data collection systems.

Notes

1. Joint United Nations Programme for HIV/AIDS. 2016. *AIDS by the Numbers 2016.* Geneva. http://www.unaids.org/en/resources/documents/2016/AIDS-by-the-numbers.

2. World Health Organization. 2016. *Global Tuberculosis Report 2016.* Geneva. http://who.int/tb/country/en/.

3. World Health Organization. 2016. *Global Health Estimates 2015: Deaths by Cause, Age and Sex, by Country and by Region, 2000–2015.* Geneva. http://www.who.int/healthinfo/global_burden_disease/en/.

4. World Health Organization. 2014. *Global Status Report on Alcohol and Health 2014.* Geneva. http://www.who.int/substance_abuse/publications/global_alcohol_report/en/.

5. These 110 countries have more than 80 percent of the world population.

6. World Health Organization. 2016. *World Health Statistics 2016: Monitoring Health for the SDGs.* Geneva. http://who.int/gho/publications/world_health_statistics/en/.

![book icon] Quality education

4 Ensure inclusive and equitable quality education and promote lifelong learning opportunities for all

The ratio of students completing lower secondary school increased in Sub-Saharan Africa from 23 percent in 1990 to 42 percent in 2014 but remains low compared with a global ratio of 75 percent. Increased enrollment at school leads to an empowered citizenry and a more productive labor force. Goal 4 aims to make learning opportunities accessible to all. It also examines the quality of education, which plays a large role in sustainable development and poverty alleviation. Investment in human capital at various ages accelerates improvement in other areas.

Measuring learning outcomes

The Programme for International Student Assessment (PISA) assesses 15-year-old students' literacy in reading, mathematics, and science (target 4.1). In 2015 success in reading was widespread, but mathematics was more challenging (figure 4a). In 9 of the 49 countries surveyed fewer than two-thirds of students attained the lowest mathematics proficiency level.

4a More students struggle to reach proficiency in mathematics than in reading
Share of 15-year-old students reaching the lowest proficiency in mathematics and reading, 2015 (%)

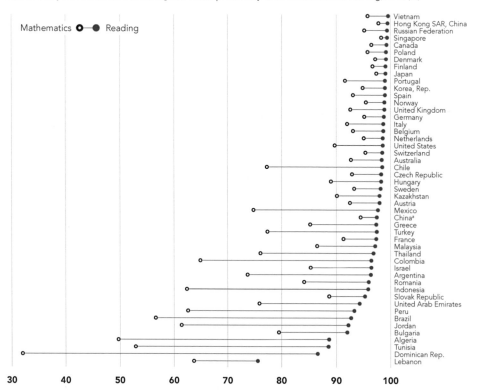

Note: Excludes countries with a population of fewer than 5 million. Data show the share of students above level 1B in reading and above level 1 in mathematics.
a. Refers to four provinces: Beijing, Guangdong, Jiangsu, and Shanghai.
Source: Organisation for Economic Co-operation and Development; World Bank EdStats database.

Literacy and numeracy are critical at all ages for individual and national development (target 4.6), but can be difficult to measure. For instance, school-based assessments do not cover children who are not attending school. The number of people who are literate or illiterate is often based on self-reported data, and some countries apply different lengths of school attendance or levels of completion to declare a person literate. The most recently available data show that around 85 percent of the world's adults have basic literacy (figure 4b). But the level and speed of achievement vary across regions and by age group.

Leaving no child behind

Ninety percent of children worldwide completed a full course of primary education in 2014, but just 75 percent went on to finish lower-secondary education (figure 4l). Access to education—ensuring learning opportunities for all children, youths, and adults, regardless of background or circumstance—has been one of the main goals of the global development agenda for more than 25 years and continues to be a priority (target 4.5).

The number of children not attending primary school was halved worldwide over the past two decades, driven by large increases in school enrollment in China and India (figure 4k). In addition, Sub-Saharan Africa reduced the number of out-of-school children by 27 percent from 47 million in 1996 (the peak) to 34 million in 2014, despite 59 percent growth in the primary school–age population over that period.

Still, around 61 million primary school–age children remained out of school in 2014—a third of them in India, Nigeria, Pakistan, and Sudan, many from poor households. In Nigeria 71 percent of children from poor households were not attending school in 2013, compared with only 5 percent of children from rich households (figure 4m). The gaps in Pakistan and India are similar.

Children in low- and middle-income countries are less likely to enroll in school as they get older (figures 4g–4j). The trend is seen across both rich and poor households, but the gap is substantial. There is also inequity in education between children from rural and urban areas in many countries: those from urban areas are almost three times more likely than children from rural areas to complete nine years of schooling in Senegal (figure 4n). And girls are disadvantaged in either case. Girls from poor households are less likely than boys from poor

4b Adult and youth literacy rates increased in all regions between 2000 and 2010
Literacy rate (%)

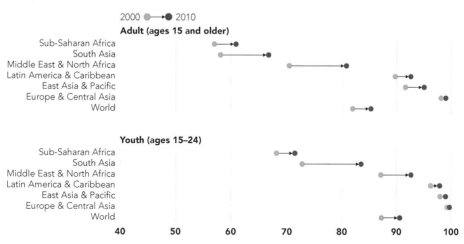

Note: The reference period is 1995–2004 for 2000 and 2005–14 for 2010.
Source: United Nations Educational, Scientific and Cultural Organization Institute for Statistics; WDI (SE.ADT. LITR.ZS, SE.ADT.1524.LT.ZS).

Primary school enrollment is near universal in most countries, but other levels are not

School enrollment by education level, most recent year available during 2013–15 (% gross)

| | 0–25 | | 25–50 | | 50–75 | | 75–100+ᵃ | | No data |

4c Preprimary

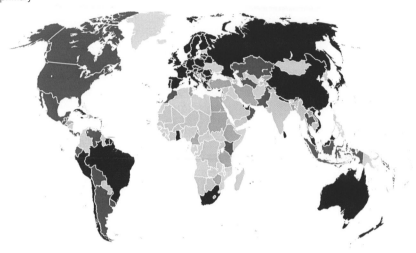

4d Primary

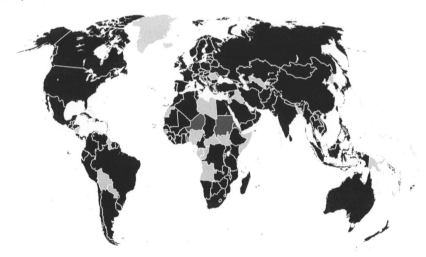

4g Low income, 2014

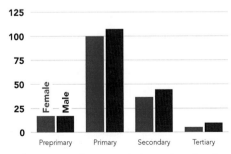

4h Lower middle income, 2014

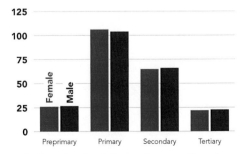

a. The gross enrollment ratio is the number of students enrolled in a given level of education, regardless of age, expressed as a percentage of the official school-age population which corresponds to the same level of education, and it may exceed 100 percent.

School enrollment by education level, most recent year available during 2013–15 (% gross)

 0–25   25–50   50–75   75–100+[a]   No data

4e Secondary

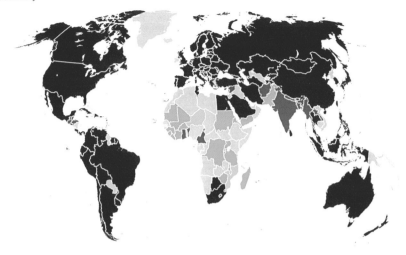

4f Tertiary

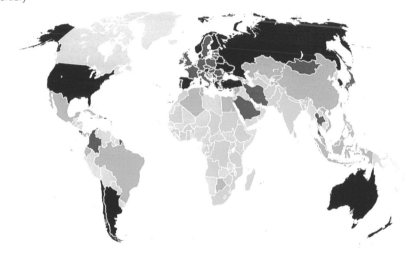

4i Upper middle income, 2014

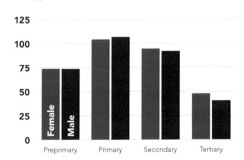

4j High income, 2014

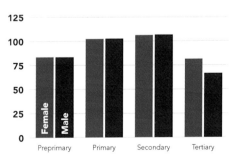

Source: United Nations Educational, Scientific and Cultural Organization Institute for Statistics; WDI (SE.PRE. ENRR, SE.PRM.ENRR, SE.SEC.ENRR, SE.TER.ENRR).

households to complete nine years of schooling; and the trend is similar for girls from rural households.

Filling the data gaps

Measuring learning achievements across the globe remains a challenge for Goal 4. While many types of learning assessments are available, different methods and varied coverages of ages, subjects, and years make comparisons across countries difficult. Also difficult is defining a "minimum competency" in different social contexts. Data availability is also a challenge. For example, the United Nations Children's Fund generates the Early Child Development Index to measure the developmental status of children, but data are available only for a few countries (target 4.2). While data disaggregated by sex and wealth quintile are available (target 4.5), parity indices for disability, ethnicity, and language are more limited.[1]

Notes

1. UNESCO Institute for Statistics (UIS). 2016. *Sustainable Development Data Digest: Laying the Foundation to Measure Sustainable Development Goal 4*. Montreal, Canada: UIS. http://www .uis.unesco.org/Education/Documents/uis-sdg4 -digest-2016.PDF.

4k The number of children out of school fell across regions
Primary school–age children out of school, by region (millions)

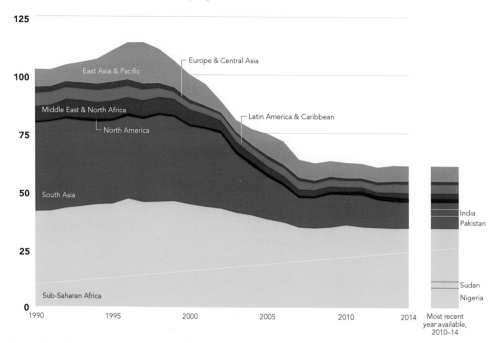

Source: United Nations Educational, Scientific and Cultural Organization Institute for Statistics; WDI (SE.PRM. UNER).

4l More children are completing primary education, but fewer finish secondary education

Primary completion rate
(% of relevant age group[1])

Lower secondary completion rate
(% of relevant age group[1])

Source: United Nations Educational, Scientific and Cultural Organization Institute for Statistics; WDI (SE.PRM.CMPT.ZS, SE.SEC.CMPT.LO.ZS).

4m Not all children have the same opportunities to enroll or remain in school

Primary school-age children out of school, by wealth quintile (% of relevant age group)

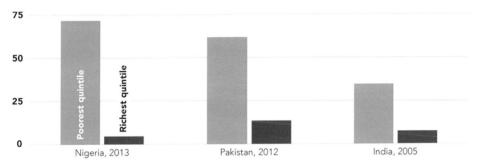

Source: Demographic and Health Surveys; World Bank EdStats.
Note: Data are for countries with the highest number of out-of-school children.

4n In Senegal students from poor households and rural areas are at a disadvantage in completing education

Proportion of 15- to 19-year-olds who completed years of education, by wealth quintile and area, Senegal, 2014 (%)

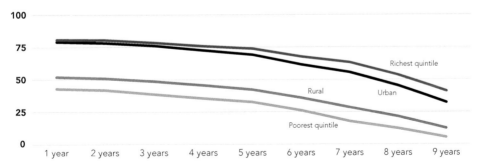

Source: World Bank EdStats estimates based on Demographic and Health Surveys.

☿ Gender equality

5 Achieve gender equality and empower all women and girls

One hundred fifty countries have at least one law that treats women and men differently, and 63 countries have five or more. Such institutional biases—together with adverse social norms, persistent gender gaps in access to assets, and the failure to recognize, reduce, and redistribute unpaid domestic work—undermine women's economic empowerment. Goal 5 offers an opportunity to deliver transformative actions for addressing these constraints and for accelerating progress toward stronger economies.

Ending legal gender differences

Ending all forms of discrimination against women and girls is crucial for inclusive sustainable development (target 5.1). Widespread legal gender differences affect women's economic prospects—for example, by making it difficult for women to own property, open bank accounts, start businesses, and enter certain professions. Countries in the Middle East and North Africa have on average 16 laws relating to employment and entrepreneurship that differentiate between women and men, while countries in South Asia average 8, and those in Sub-Saharan Africa average 6 (figure 5a).[1,2] In East Asia and Pacific, the average number of legal gender differences is 5, followed by Europe and Central Asia with 3, Latin America and the Caribbean with 2, and North America with 1.

5a Employment and entrepreneurship related legal gender differences are widespread
Number of employment and entrepreneurship related laws differentiating between women and men

| ■ 0 | ▦ 1–4 | ▦ 5–14 | ■ 15–29 | ▨ No data |

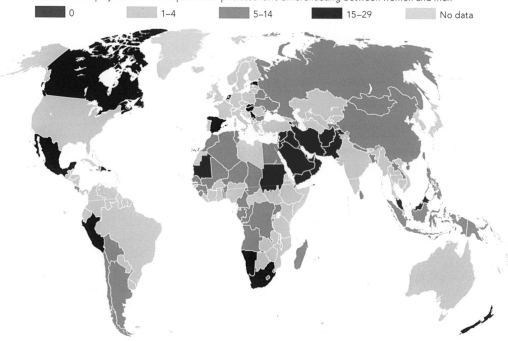

Source: World Bank Group, 2015, *Women, Business, and the Law 2016: Getting to Equal*, Washington, DC.

Combating harmful social norms

Despite the existence of violence against women across the globe, specific laws against gender-based violence are not universal (target 5.2). In 49 countries there is no specific law against domestic violence, in 45 there is no legislation to address sexual harassment, and 112 countries do not criminalize marital rape. And in many countries societal norms permit physical and verbal abuse—for instance, if a wife argues with her husband or partner, refuses to have sex, burns food, goes out without telling him, or neglects the children (figure 5b). In Timor-Leste and Central African Republic, for example, the law penalizes domestic violence, sexual harassment and marital rape, but around 80 percent of women still justify spousal abuse in any of the five circumstances listed. While recent laws to address gender-based violence signal progress over the past couple of years, social norms against wider gender equality reduce the potential for change.

Breaking the cycle of early marriage and poverty

A woman's access to education and later her employment opportunities as well as the nature and terms of her work are often compromised by early marriage: Goal 5 looks to eliminate this practice (target 5.3). Young married girls whose schooling is cut short often lack the knowledge and skills for formal work and are limited to occupations with lower incomes and inferior working conditions (figure 5c). Early marriage is widespread in parts of South Asia, Sub-Saharan Africa, the Middle East and North Africa, and Latin America and the Caribbean. Even though Niger, Chad, Central African Republic, and Mali legally prohibit child marriage, and there are penalties for authorizing or knowingly entering into early marriage, more than half of all girls are married by age 18.[3]

Promoting shared responsibility for unpaid work

Women typically spend disproportionately more time on unpaid domestic and care work than men. Goal 5 seeks recognition of this work and a more equitable distribution of these activities between women and men (target 5.4). Of the countries surveyed, women spend on average between 13 (Thailand) and 28 percent (Mexico) of their time in unpaid domestic and care activities, while men spend between 3 (Japan) and 13 percent (Sweden) (figure 5d).[4] This unequal division of responsibilities is correlated with gender differences in economic opportunities, including low female labor force participation, occupational sex segregation, and earnings differentials.

5b Women are more likely to tolerate domestic abuse in countries with fewer legal provisions against domestic violence
Share of women believing a man is justified in beating his wife for different reasons, by number of legal provisions in a country against domestic violence (%)

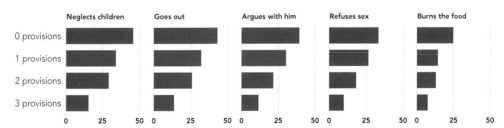

Note: The number of legal provisions ranges between 0 and 3 depending on the existence of a law on domestic violence, sexual harassment or marital rape. (yes = 1, no = 0).
Source: Demographic and Health Surveys (DHS), Multiple Indicator Cluster Surveys (MICS), and other surveys, most recent year available during 2009–15; World Bank Group, 2015, *Women, Business and the Law 2016: Getting to Equal*, Washington, DC; WDI (SG.VAW.NEGL.ZS, SG.VAW.REFU.ZS, SG.VAW.GOES.ZS, SG.VAW.BURN.ZS, SG.VAW.ARGU.ZS, SG.LEG.DVAW); World Bank Gender Statistics database (SG.LEG.DVAW, SG.LEG.MRRP, SG.LEG.SXHR). Aggregations based on available data from 54 countries.

5c Early marriage correlates with women in inferior working conditions

Vulnerable employment female (unpaid family workers or own-account workers, % of female employment)

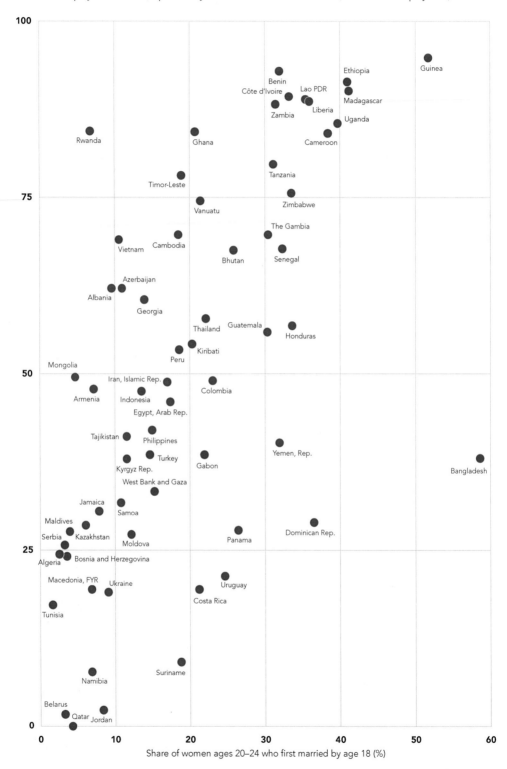

Share of women ages 20–24 who first married by age 18 (%)

Source: Demographic and Health Surveys, Multiple Indicator Cluster Surveys, and other surveys ;
International Labour Organization Key Indicators of the Labour Market database; WDI (SP.M18.2024.FE.ZS,
SL.EMP.VULN.FE.ZS), most recent year available during 2009–15.

5d Women spend more time on unpaid work than men

Share of total time allocated to unpaid domestic and care work, countries for which data are available (%)

5e Differences persist between men and women's Internet use

Difference between the percentage of female and male population using the Internet (percentage points)

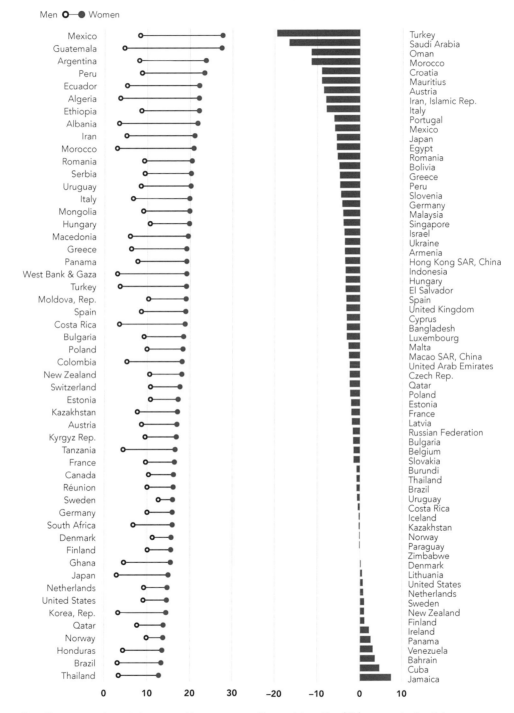

Men ○—● Women

Note: Data may not be strictly comparable across countries as the methods and sampling involved for data collection may differ. Figure displays most recent year available during 2009–15.
Source: United Nations Statistical Division.

Source: International Telecommunication Union, most recent year available during 2012–15.

5f In most countries women dominate in health and education studies and men in engineering and science studies
Share of countries where the field of study is female- or male-dominated (%)

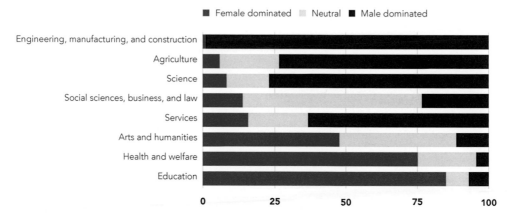

Note: A given tertiary education program is "female dominated" if the female share of enrollment in the program is 5 percentage points higher than female share of tertiary graduates, "male dominated" if female share of enrollment in the program is 5 percentage points less than female share of tertiary graduates, and neutral if the difference between female share of enrollment in the program and female share of tertiary graduates is less than 5 percentage points. The country sample size for each field of study ranges from 101 to 115.
Source: Estimations based on UNESCO Institute for Statistics; Education Statistics database UIS.FEP.56.F600, UIS.FEP.56.F140, UIS.FEP.56.F500, UIS.FEP.56.F700, UIS.FEP.56.F200,UIS.FEP.56.F400, UIS.FEP.56.F800, UIS. FEP.56.F300, SE.TER.GRAD.FE.ZS, most recent year available during 2012–15.

Enhancing women's use of technology

Technology can contribute to women's empowerment by helping them overcome mobility constraints, access relevant information and new communication channels, and participate in existing networks (target 5.b).

Widespread differences between men and women in access to basic technology persist in most parts of the world (figure 5e). Overall, women are less likely to be Internet users regardless of their region or income. The difference in Internet use can be as high as 20 percentage points (Turkey). Only one-fifth of countries with data have no evidence of a difference.[5]

Technology also presents an opportunity to increase financial inclusion. While only 2.5 percent of men and 1.6 percent of women worldwide have a mobile money account, 12.8 percent of men and 10.3 percent of women in Sub-Saharan Africa have one. Although financial inclusion starts with having a bank account, only with regular use do people benefit from it. Around 40 percent of wage recipients in low- and middle-income countries

report receiving their wage payments into an account, and large gender gaps remain. Women in low- and middle-income countries are about a third less likely than men to report having received any wage payments into an account in the previous year.[4]

Expanding female participation in nontraditional areas

Teaching both women and men the technical skills and capabilities to succeed in the digital economy is a top priority. Across the world, women are overrepresented in education and health; equally represented in social sciences, business, and law; and underrepresented in engineering, manufacturing, construction, and science (figure 5f). This sharp divergence does not reflect the capabilities of men and women in different subjects. Driving this segregation are gender biases at school and at home, limited exposure of girls to science and technology at an early age, and a lack of opportunities to enroll in such programs. Early exposure can shift stereotypes that discourage girls from participating in science and technology fields, with implications for their occupational choices and earning potential.

Increasing women's representation in parliaments

Goal 5 strives for the full participation of women at all levels of decisionmaking in political, economic, and public life (target 5.5). Across the globe women occupy, on average, 23 percent of parliamentary seats in 2016, up from 12 percent in 1997. Women made up nearly 29 percent of seats in Latin America and the Caribbean and 26 percent in Europe and Central Asia. Despite a fourfold increase in the share of women parliamentarians in the Middle East and North Africa since 1997, the region still had the lowest proportion of women-held seats, at 17 percent. In 2016, only two countries had 50 percent or more women in parliament: Rwanda, with nearly 64 percent, and Bolivia, with 53 percent. In contrast, seven countries had no women in parliament: Yemen, Vanuatu, Tonga, Qatar, Palau, Micronesia, and Haiti (figure 5g).

Notes

1. *Women, Business, and the Law* examines 21 differences in policies for unmarried women and 26 for married women (or 47 questions in the database) that affect women's economic opportunities.

2. The measure of legal gender differences can sum to a whole number or a decimal for any economy because the question on job restrictions has 10 subquestions that examine specific restrictions on women's work. Each subquestion thus has a value of one-tenth. Values presented here are rounded to the nearest whole number.

3. The legal age of marriage for boys and girls is 21 years in Niger and Chad, and 18 in the Central African Republic. In Mali, the legal age is 18 years for boys and 16 years for girls.

4. Demirguc-Kunt, A., L. Klapper, D. Singer, and P. Van Oudheusden. 2015. "The Global Findex Database 2014: Measuring Financial Inclusion around the World". Policy Research Working Paper 7255. World Bank, Washington, DC. Each economy is classified based on the classification of World Bank Group's fiscal year 2015 (July 1, 2014–June 30, 2015).

5. There is no evidence of a gap when the difference in the use of Internet between men and women is ±1 percentage point.

5g Women remain underrepresented in national parliaments in most countries
Proportion of seats held by women in national parliaments (percent), 2016

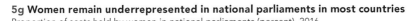

0–15   15–30   30–45   More than 45   No data

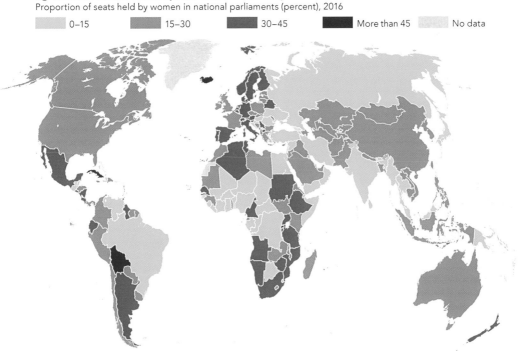

Source: Inter-Parliamentary Union (http://www.ipu.org); WDI (SG.GEN.PARL.ZS).

Clean water and sanitation

6 Ensure availability and sustainable management of water and sanitation for all

More than 90 percent of the world's people now have access to improved water sources. In the past 25 years 2.1 billion people gained access to improved sanitation facilities. At the same time the share of people practicing open defecation halved, from 27 percent to 13 percent. While such improvements show progress toward access for all, these measures do not capture all dimensions of providing water and sanitation. Goal 6 introduces a new, more comprehensive monitoring framework to ensure access that is safe, equitable, and universal.

Expanding access to drinking water and sanitation

Until recently countries reported their populations' access to water and sanitation by distinguishing between "improved" and "unimproved" coverage. In 2015, 663 million people were drinking from unimproved sources such as unprotected dug wells, and 2.4 billion lacked improved sanitation facilities. The bulk of those without were in Sub-Saharan Africa and South Asia (see figures 6d and 6e on page 34), where rural dwellers, especially the poorest, lagged behind others in access to both water and sanitation (figures 6a, 6b, 6f and 6g).

Measuring access more comprehensively

Goal 6 commits to universal access to water, sanitation, and hygiene under a new, broader, and more refined monitoring framework (targets 6.1 and 6.2). The unimproved–improved distinction is replaced by "safely managed" services. For water, this requires that the household's drinking water source is on premises, available when needed, and free of fecal and locally relevant chemical contaminants. For sanitation, emphasis is on the links in the sanitation chain from initial defecation through waste management (including containment, disposal, and transport of human excreta), and on the availability of an appropriate handwashing facility. Monitoring these components and inequalities will help assess progress toward the longer term aim of universal access.

Household surveys will increasingly measure these new components, but at present, data are limited. Available data show how the refined methodology can affect measures

6a The number of people without access to an improved water source is declining
Number of people without access to an improved water source (billions)

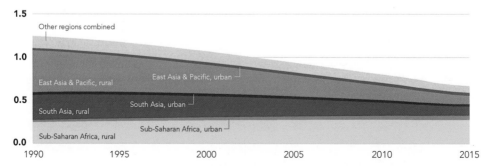

Source: World Health Organization/United Nations Children's Fund Joint Monitoring Programme for Water Supply and Sanitation; WDI (SH.H2O.SAFE.RU.ZS, SH.H2O.SAFE.UR.ZS, SP.URB.TOTL, SP.RUR.TOTL).

6b 2.4 billion people still lack access to improved sanitation facilities

Number of people without access to improved sanitation facilities (billions)

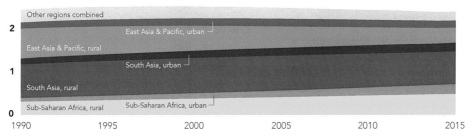

Source: World Health Organization/United Nations Children's Fund Joint Monitoring Programme for Water Supply and Sanitation; WDI (SH.STA.ACSN.RU, SH.STA.ACSN.UR, SP.URB.TOTL, SP.RUR.TOTL).

of access. For example, in Niger 66 percent of the population has access to an improved source of water, but new data show that only 10 percent have access on premises (figure 6c). Those without on-premise access must plan ahead to collect water, an exercise that can take up to 30 minutes (the threshold for "basic water"—another measure sometimes used) or even longer (improved, but not basic).

Even if data are not yet available on all aspects of safely managed water, there generally is information on improved water on premises, and access to safely managed water can be no higher than that. On average across six countries, 60 percent of urban dwellers and 75 percent of rural dwellers previously classified as having access would now be considered to be without access. When other new requirements

of access are considered, the shares are likely to fall further.[1] These refined measures can help quantify major issues invisible in previous definitions.

Incorporating handwashing in the definition of sanitation access has a similar impact. A 54-country study found that the handwashing criterion was unmet for between 4 percent (Serbia, and Bosnia and Herzegovina) and 99 percent (Liberia and Ethiopia) of the population.[2] In another study of 10 countries, access to cleansing materials—fundamental to women for menstrual hygiene management—was below 25 percent in more than half the countries.[3] Such data[4] can give new insights to sanitation challenges facing different populations and enable countries and the international community to refine and focus service provision.[5]

6c Under stricter definitions, fewer people have access to water

Share of population at each access level, according to latest dataset, by country (%)

■ Improved water source[a]　■ Basic water[b]　■ Improved water on premises　**?** Safely managed water[c]

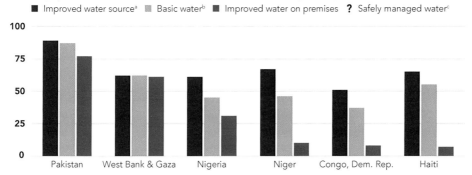

a. Differs from the WDI indicator SH.H2O.SAFE.ZS, which is based on multiple surveys.
b. Improved water source, with no more than a 30-minute round-trip collection time.
c. Safely managed water access has not yet been assessed and is not shown but can be no greater than improved water on premises.
Source: World Bank WASH Poverty Diagnostics 2016.

6d Those who lack improved water sources are concentrated largely in Sub-Saharan Africa
Share of population with access to an improved water source, 2015 (%)

| | 0–25 | | 25–50 | | 50–75 | | 75–100 | | No data |

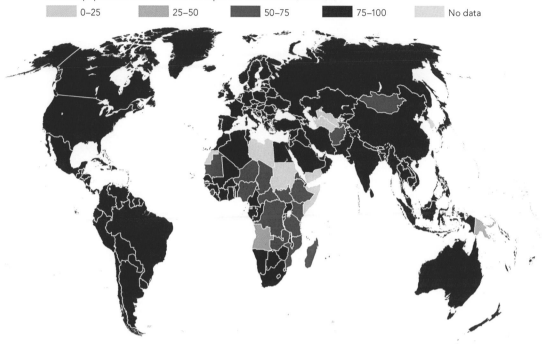

Source: World Health Organization/United Nations Children's Fund Joint Monitoring Programme for Water Supply and Sanitation; WDI (SH.H2O.SAFE.ZS).

6e Access to improved sanitation facilities is lacking in some countries in South Asia and Sub-Saharan Africa
Share of population with access to improved sanitation facilities, 2015 (%)

| | 0–25 | | 25–50 | | 50–75 | | 75–100 | | No data |

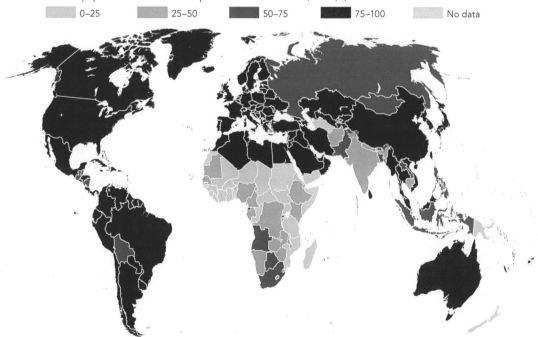

Source: World Health Organization/United Nations Children's Fund Joint Monitoring Programme for Water Supply and Sanitation; WDI (SH.STA.ACSN).

6f The poorest people in rural areas suffer from especially low access to water...

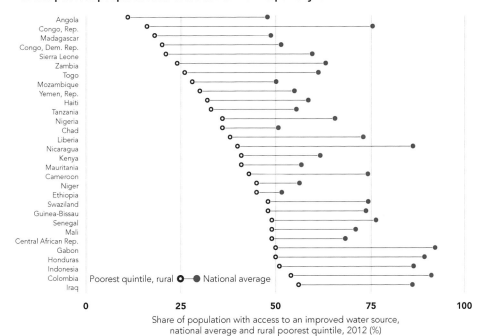

Poorest quintile, rural ◯—● National average

Share of population with access to an improved water source,
national average and rural poorest quintile, 2012 (%)

Source: World Health Organization/United Nations Children's Fund Joint Monitoring Programme for Water
Supply and Sanitation; WDI (SH.H2O.SAFE.ZS); Health, Nutrition, and Population Statistics by Wealth Quintile
(SH.H2O.SAFE.RU.Q1.ZS).

6g ...and to sanitation

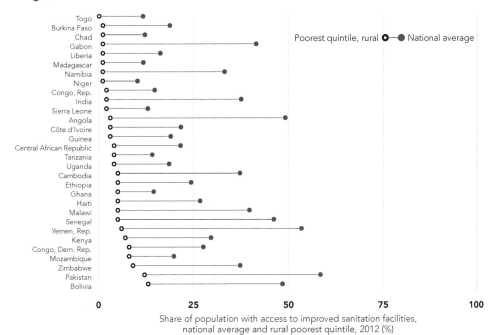

Poorest quintile, rural ◯—● National average

Share of population with access to improved sanitation facilities,
national average and rural poorest quintile, 2012 (%)

Source: World Health Organization/United Nations Children's Fund Joint Monitoring Programme for Water
Supply and Sanitation; WDI (SH.STA.ACSN); Health, Nutrition, and Population Statistics by Wealth Quintile
(SH.STA.ACSN.RU.Q1.ZS).

6h Open defecation is widespread throughout parts of South Asia and Sub-Saharan Africa
Number of people practicing open defecation, 2015

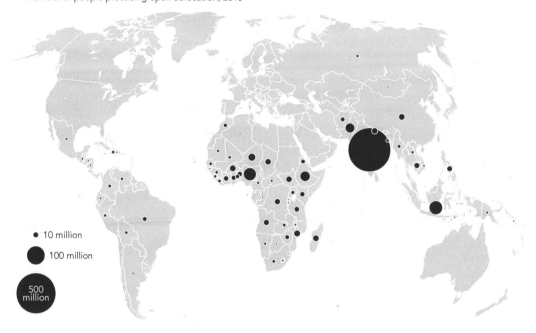

- ● 10 million
- ⬤ 100 million
- ⬤ 500 million

Source: World Health Organization/United Nations Children's Fund Joint Monitoring Programme for Water Supply and Sanitation; WDI (SH.STA.ODFC.ZS, SP.POP.TOTL).

Ending open defecation

The elimination of open defecation is an urgent priority (target 6.2). In 2015, an estimated 946 million people defecated in the open—for example, outside in street gutters, behind bushes, or into open bodies of water (figure 6h). This contaminates drinking water sources and spreads deadly diseases such as cholera, diarrhea, and dysentery. Open defecation is particularly acute among the rural poor in South Asia and Sub-Saharan Africa.

Addressing the entire water cycle

Goal 6 recognizes that sustainably managing water goes beyond simply providing a safe water supply and sanitation, as it addresses broader water cycle issues of water quality and wastewater (target 6.3); water use and scarcity (target 6.4); water resource management (target 6.5); and ecosystems (target 6.6). All these issues influence access, particularly for regions facing increasingly frequent extreme weather events due to climate change, urbanization pressures, and shifting pollution patterns.

Globally, water supplies per person halved over the past 50 years, and water shortages affect many countries (figure 6i). Ninety percent of water withdrawals in low-income countries went to agriculture in 2014, while industry had the highest share in high-income countries (44%).

Monitoring and managing water resources

Managing and assessing water resources rely on incorporating new data sources, such as satellite measures of aquifer levels. Increased analytical precision, integration of information and of national programs, and multinational cooperation are critical to improve monitoring and translate global ambitions into national action.

This will require increased participation by local communities and other stakeholders (acknowledged in target 6.b). Of 94 countries in a recent UN survey round, 83 percent reported having clearly defined procedures for stakeholder participation in water, sanitation, and hygiene planning, but fewer than half had even "moderate" implementation.[6]

6i Many countries already withdraw a very high proportion of their available water
Total annual freshwater withdrawals, by country, 2014 (% of internal renewable freshwater resources)

| ▨ 0–25 | ▨ 25–75 | ▨ 75+[a] | ▨ No data |

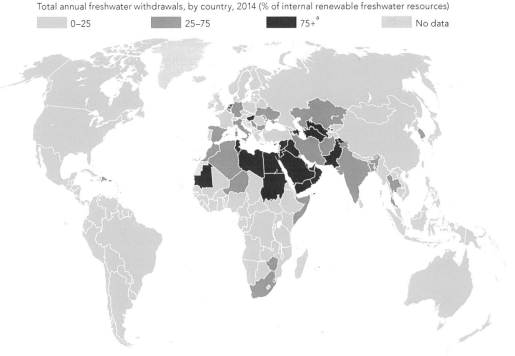

a. Withdrawals can exceed 100 percent due to extraction from nonrenewable aquifers, desalination, or water reuse. For example, in Bahrain, Egypt, Turkmenistan, and United Arab Emirates withdrawals exceed 1,000 percent.
Source: Food and Agriculture Organization; WDI (ER.H2O.FWTL.ZS).

Improved water management should be seen in context. Advances in equitable access to water and sanitation contribute to progress in health, nutrition, food security, gender equality, disaster resilience, environmental sustainability, and many other areas.[7] For example, access to water, sanitation, and handwashing contributes to inclusive and effective school learning environments, promoting the goal of quality education for all.[8]

Notes

1. The Water Supply, Sanitation, and Hygiene (WASH) Poverty Diagnostic has been working to examine the implications of adopting the new measurements of access.

2. WHO/UNICEF Joint Monitoring Programme (JMP) for Water Supply and Sanitation, 2015, *Progress on Sanitation and Drinking Water—2015 Update and MDG Assessment.*

3. Loughnan, L., Bain, R., Rop, R., Sommer, M., and Slaymaker, T. 2016. "What Can Existing Data on Water and Sanitation Tell Us About Menstrual Hygiene Management?" *Waterlines* 35(3).

4. The most comprehensive assessment of the baseline global situation under these new measurements will be released by the World Health Organization/United Nations Children's Fund Joint Monitoring Programme in 2017–18.

5. World Bank WASH Poverty Diagnostic 2016.

6. UN-Water. 2016. *Integrated Monitoring Guide for SDG 6 Targets and Global Indicators.* Geneva.

7. Integrated monitoring of water and sanitation related SDG targets – GEMI: http://www.unwater.org/gemi/.

8. Indicators for target 4.a—see United Nations Economic and Social Council 2015 *Report of the Inter-Agency and Expert Group on Sustainable Development Goal.*

☀ Affordable and clean energy

7 Ensure access to affordable, reliable, sustainable, and modern energy for all

Nearly 1.1 billion people had no access to electricity in 2014, and more than 3 billion had no access to clean fuels and technologies. Goal 7 recognizes that extending access to electricity and other forms of energy is fundamental to improving people's lives and communities. It aims for efficiencies in energy use and the promotion of renewable sources to sustainably manage resources for development.

Easing daily life through access to energy

Modern energy improves many areas of daily life. Better sanitation systems, well functioning health care and education services, and dependable transportation and telecommunications all depend on reliable electricity. Lighting a single room allows a child to read or do homework at night, while continuous power can support larger appliances, keep food cold, and allow businesses to flourish. Other alternatives, where they exist, often have significant health or pollution risks. Emissions from inefficient household energy sources like kerosene and traditional biomass can directly contribute to diseases and premature mortality among the poorest people, who have little or no access to health care. Goal 7 seeks to expand access to affordable, reliable, and modern energy services to all (target 7.1).

Expanding access to electricity

In 2014 around 15 percent of the world's population had no access to electricity (figures 7d and 7e). Nearly half were in rural areas of Sub-Saharan Africa, and nearly a third were rural dwellers in South Asia. In all, 86 percent of people without electricity lived in rural areas, where providing infrastructure is more challenging. Of the remainder in urban areas, most were in Sub-Saharan Africa (figure 7a).

Electrification has expanded in all regions and in both urban and rural areas. South Asia has driven global declines in the share of the rural population without access to electricity, with just 28 percent of rural dwellers lacking electricity in 2014, compared with 68 percent in 1991, while the urban rate fell from 18 percent to 3 percent.

7a Globally, the number of people without access to electricity is falling
People without access to electricity (billions)

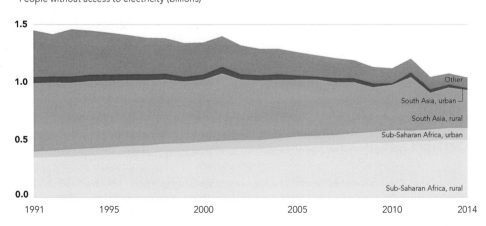

Source: Sustainable Energy for All; WDI (EG.ELC.ACCS.RU.ZS, EG.ELC.ACCS.UR.ZS, SP.RUR.TOTL, SP.URB.TOTL).

In most regions, electrification has outpaced population growth. An exception is Sub-Saharan Africa, where electrification has not kept up with population growth: 154 million more people in rural areas lacked access in 2014 than in 1991. Similarly, the number of people in urban areas without access rose from 58 million in 1991 to about 108 million in 2014.

Converting to clean cooking fuels

Clean cooking fuels and technologies are in many cases less hazardous to health and the environment than their alternatives. In 2014 more than 40 percent of the global population—mostly in South Asia, East Asia and Pacific, and Sub-Saharan Africa—had no access to these fuels (figure 7b).

Access to clean cooking fuels and technologies has not expanded as fast as access to electricity. In South Asia 77 percent of people did not have access to these fuels in 2000. While that share dropped to 68 percent by 2014 (figure 7c), it was insufficient to keep up

7b More than 3 billion people still lack access to clean cooking fuels and technologies
People without access to clean cooking fuels and technologies (billions)

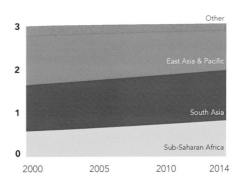

Source: Sustainable Energy for All; WDI (EG.CFT. ACCS.ZS, SP.POP.TOTL).

with population growth, leaving an additional 91 million people without access.

Access has improved in East Asia and Pacific —both in terms of population share and number of people affected. Over half of all people did not have access to clean cooking fuels

7c Access to clean cooking fuels is lowest in Sub-Saharan Africa, but China and India also have large populations without access
Share of population with access to clean cooking fuels and technologies, 2014 (%)

| 0–33 | 33–67 | 67–100 | No data |

Source: Sustainable Energy for All; WDI (EG.CFT.ACCS.ZS).

7d Access to electricity is lowest in Sub-Saharan Africa...

Access to electricity, 2014 (% of population)

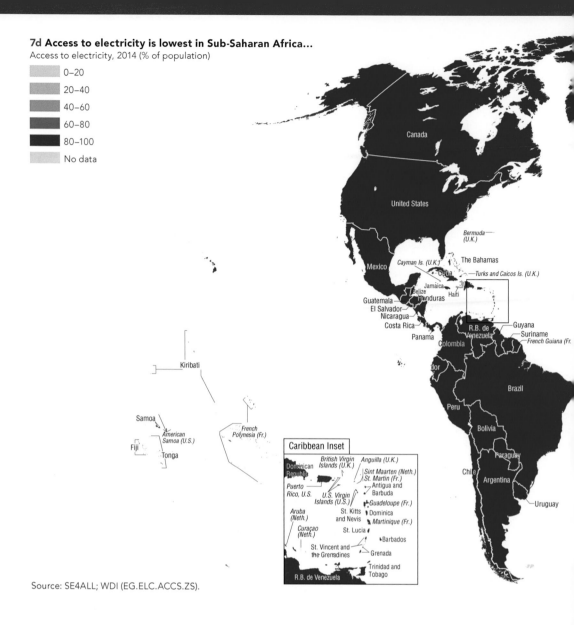

Source: SE4ALL; WDI (EG.ELC.ACCS.ZS).

7e ...but substantial populations in India and Bangladesh also lack access

People without access to electricity, 2014 (%)

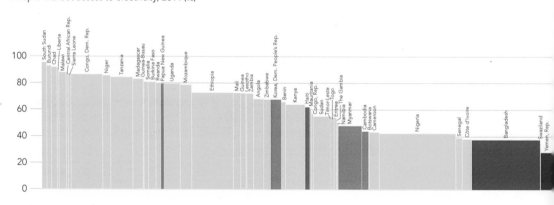

Countries with less than 80 percent access to electricity and a population of at least 1 million (scaled by population)

Source: SE4ALL; WDI (EG.ELC.ACCS.ZS, SP.POP.TOTL).

Europe Inset

India

■ East Asia & Pacific　■ Latin America & Caribbean　■ Middle East & North Africa　■ South Asia　■ Sub-Saharan Africa

and technologies in 2000; in 2014 this share dropped to 42 percent. Despite a rise in the total population of 11 percent, 206 million fewer people lacked access than 14 years earlier.

A large population rise and a negligible fall in the percentage of people lacking access to clean cooking fuels and technologies in Sub-Saharan Africa (from 87 percent in 2000 to 86 percent in 2014) means that, in 2014, 250 million more people lacked access than in 2000.

Measuring modern energy access in new ways

Energy access is currently measured through a simple binary indicator: either a house, village, or facility is connected to a power grid or it is not. But a connection does not mean that electricity is always available and affordable. Conversely, advances in low-cost and effective off-grid systems now mean that a grid connection may not be necessary to enjoy some important benefits of modern energy. These innovations are particularly relevant for the many people without access to electricity in rural areas, where traditional grid expansion is most costly.

The measurement framework for energy access is under revision. It will eventually take into account many aspects of energy delivery, such

as the source and its capacity, the duration of access and its reliability, the quality of energy delivered (such as voltage), the affordability of access, and the legality of the energy provision. Access to electricity will be defined in five tiers: tier 1 encompasses basic lighting and phone charging; tier 2 includes a television and electric fan; tier 3 includes the use of low-intensity and discontinuous thermal or mechanical applications, such as washing machines or food processors; and tiers 4 and 5 enable heavier and continuous applications, such as air-conditioning and space heating.[1] It is likely that many people now counted as having access to electricity will fall in the lower tiers; but others with off-grid power may reach tiers 1 or 2, despite currently being counted as not having access.

Shifting to renewable energy

Goal 7 promotes more use of renewable energy to counter dependence on unsustainable, nonrenewable sources (target 7.2). The share of renewables in the global energy mix stood at just under 19 percent in 2014.

However, this is uneven across regions: the renewable share in the Middle East and North Africa stands at 1.8 percent, while the share in North America is under 10.5 percent. Sub-Saharan Africa has the highest share of renewables in its energy use—over 70 percent—while South Asia records 40 percent. These

7f Wind and solar photovoltaic account for the majority of renewables' electricity capacity added each year
Electricity generation capacity added per year, by renewable source (gigawatts)

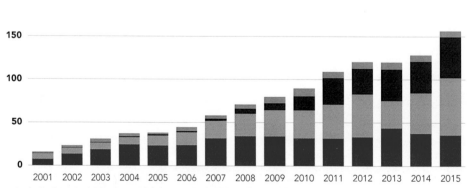

a. Includes biomass, concentrated solar power, geothermal, and ocean.
Source: International Renewable Energy Agency.

high shares reflect the practice in many low- and lower-middle-income countries of reliance on traditional biomass for fuel.

For the first time, renewables accounted for more than half of net annual additions to power capacity globally and overtook coal in terms of cumulative installed capacity in the world.[2] Of the renewables, hydropower accounts for over 60 percent of total capacity, but wind and solar photovoltaic are now dominating the new capacity added each year (figure 7f).

Driving energy efficiency

Goal 7 aims to double the global rate of improvement in energy efficiency (target 7.3). Energy efficiency refers to the amount of output that can be produced by using a given amount of energy—for example, kilometers traveled per liter of fuel. A related economywide measure, energy intensity, reflects the amount of energy required to produce a certain value of output. As energy efficiency increases, energy intensity declines, though the decline also reflects other factors, such as changing patterns of production and consumption. Global energy intensity was around 5.8 megajoules

per purchasing power parity dollar of output in 2010—that is, each dollar of output required an energy input equivalent to 0.18 liters of gasoline. This decline was from 7.6 megajoules per dollar in 1990, an average decline over the two decades of around 1.34 percent a year.

By 2014 global energy intensity had fallen further, to 5.4 megajoules per dollar, accelerating the annual decline to 1.9 percent—but still short of the target of 2.6 percent (which would amount to a doubling of the world decline over 1990–2010). However, 7 of the 20 largest energy consumers did achieve the target, showing that decoupling growth from energy use is possible in both high-income countries and emerging economies (figure 7g).

Notes

1. ESMAP (Energy Sector Management Assistance Program). 2015. *Beyond Connections: Energy Access Redefined.* ESMAP Technical Report 008/15. Washington, DC: World Bank Group. https://openknowledge.worldbank.org/handle/10986/24368.

2. World Bank, Global Tracking Framework 2017.

7g Seven of the highest energy-consuming economies exceeded 2.6 percent annual decline from 2010 to 2014

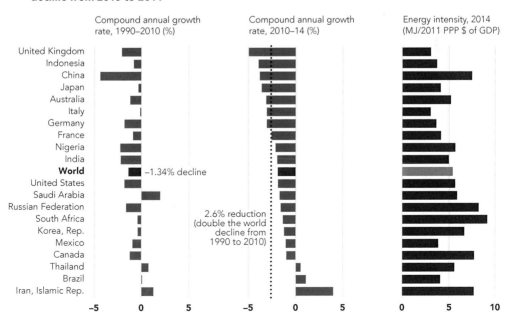

Note: Top 20 economies by energy consumption in 2014.
Source: OECD/IEA, IEA World Energy Balances; WDI (EG.EGY.PRIM.PP.KD).

Decent work and economic growth

8 Promote sustained, inclusive, and sustainable economic growth, full and productive employment, and decent work for all

Young people ages 15–24—who make up 22 percent of the world's adult population—often face great challenges in finding employment. And even after they find work, they are disproportionately engaged in low-productivity and low-quality jobs, with few opportunities. In addition to sustained job creation, Goal 8 recognizes that decoupling economic growth from environmental degradation is fundamental to sustainable development.

Getting people into jobs

Goal 8 aims at full employment for all age groups and identifies work, education, and training for young people as part of that aim (targets 8.5 and 8.6). The world's population is young: 42 percent is under age 25. In South Asia and Sub-Saharan Africa the number of people ages 15–24 has been steadily rising, to 525 million in 2015—almost half the global youth population (figure 8a). Jobs for young people are important for several reasons: they are an important vehicle for the social, economic, and political inclusion of groups and individuals, and a lack of jobs can lead to discontent and unrest among disaffected young people.[1] Moreover, an individual's first job tends to set a precedent for lifelong earnings, and those with poor job prospects risk falling into "low-pay traps."[2]

8a The youth population is growing sharply in regions with high poverty
Youth population, ages 15–24 (millions)

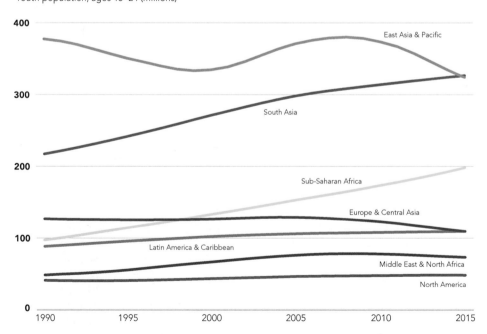

Source: World Bank staff estimates based on the United Nations Population Division's World Population Prospects; World Bank Health, Nutrition, and Population database (SP.POP.1519.FE, SP.POP.1519.MA, SP.POP.2024.FE, SP.POP.2024.MA).

8b Young people are less likely to seek work—and less likely to find it when they do
Labor force status, 2014 (% of population)

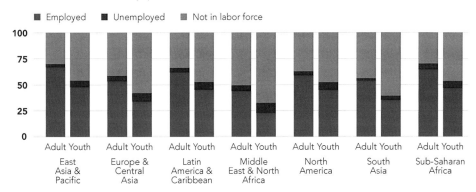

Note: *Adult* refers to people ages 15 and older, and *youth* refers to people ages 15–24.
Source: International Labour Organization Key Indicators of the Labour Market database; WDI (SL.EMP.1524.
SP.ZS, SL.EMP.TOTL.SP.ZS, SL.UEM.1524.ZS, SL.UEM.TOTL.ZS, SL.TLF.ACTI.1524.ZS, SL.TLF.TOTL.IN, SP.POP.
TOTL); World Bank Health, Nutrition, and Population database (SP.POP.1519.FE, SP.POP.1519.MA, SP.POP.2024.
FE, SP.POP.2024.MA, SP.POP.1564.TO, SP.POP.65UP.TO).

Sixty percent of young people ages 15–24 worldwide are jobless. Less than a quarter of young people in the Middle East and North Africa and a third in Europe and Central Asia —considerably less than the percentage of adults—have a job. Because young people are often involved in education and training, they are more likely than adults to be out of the labor force (figure 8b). But these gaps also reflect the fact that the youth unemployment rate is higher than the total unemployment rate in every region (figure 8e).

In many middle-income countries, a high proportion of young people are not in employment, education, or training. Neither working nor developing their productive skills for the future, this group represents a lost opportunity. Young women are much more likely than men to fall into this group, and a gender gap persists in countries at all incomes (figure 8c). The low activity of women is the result of several factors, including their primary role in households and families as well as societal norms that limit their participation in working life.

Expanding productive job opportunities for youth

Young people in low-income countries are more likely to have jobs than young people in middle- and high-income countries. Compelled to help support their families, many drop out of school prematurely and end up in precarious and low productivity employment, with few opportunities for advancement. They are often disproportionately in agricultural activities, which tend to have lower labor productivity and offer lower earnings and profits than do industry and services. And in many countries they are more likely than adults to be in unpaid work, contributing to family household enterprises (figure 8d).

Increasing growth in the Least Developed Countries

Economic growth drives development by providing more resources for better education; improved health; expanded transport, water, and energy infrastructure, and higher personal consumption. Economies grow as work and workers become more productive. Achieving persistently high growth is not easy, and few of the Least Developed Countries consistently reach 7 percent average annual GDP growth (target 8.1). In addition, many countries are growing in unsustainable ways—achieving economic growth at the expense of existing resources, shifting the burden of environmental degradation and damage to the health and well-being of a future citizenry.

8c Young women are more likely than young men to be economically inactive and not in school

Share of female youth population (ages 15–24) not in employment, education, or training, most recent year available during 2010–14 (%)

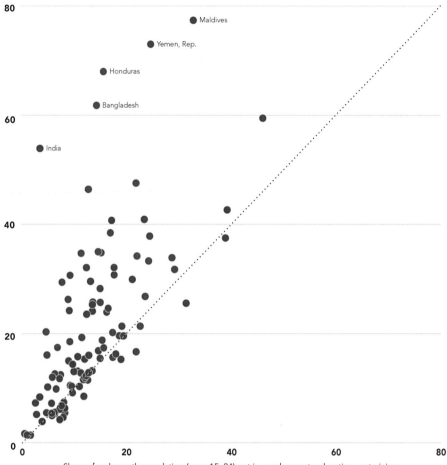

Share of male youth population (ages 15–24) not in employment, education, or training, most recent year available during 2010–14 (%)

Source: International Labour Organization Key Indicators of the Labour Market database; WDI (SL.UEM.NEET. FE.ZS, SL.UEM.NEET.MA.ZS).

8d In some countries a much larger share of youth than adults are in unpaid work

Share of employed workers who are unpaid, 20 countries with largest gap between youth (ages 15–24) and working age (ages 25–59), 2011–15 (%)

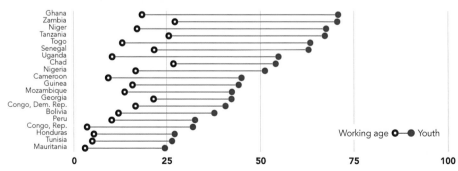

Source: World Bank Atlas of Social Protection Indicators of Resilience and Equity database.

8e Globally, youth unemployment rates are higher than adult rates

Total unemployment, 2014 (% of labor force ages 15 and older)

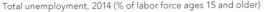

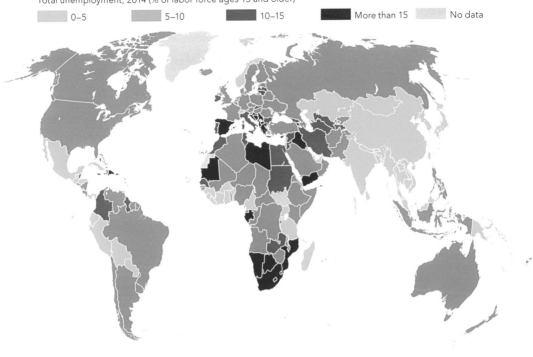

Youth unemployment, 2014 (% of labor force ages 15–24)

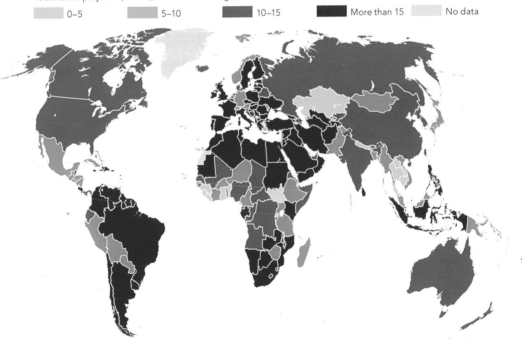

Source: International Labour Organization, Key Indicators of the Labour Market database; WDI (SL.UEM.TOTL.ZS, SL.UEM.1524.ZS).

8f Very few countries show strong decoupling of environmental degradation from economic growth

Average annual change in environmental degradation in real U.S. dollar terms, 1990–2015 (%)

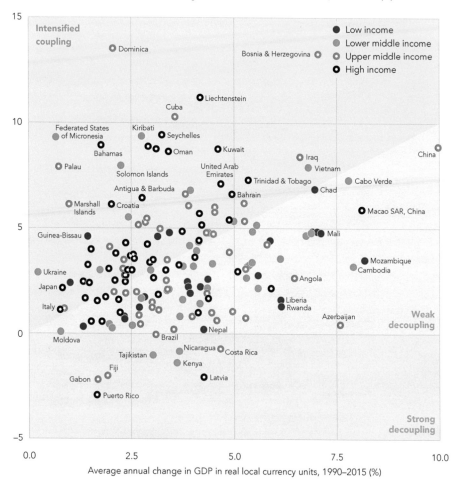

Note: Data are available for 178 countries.
Source: World Bank staff estimates using data from sources in endnote 3.

Goal 8 calls for decoupling environmental degradation from growth (target 8.4). One way to measure decoupling is to compare the rates of change in environmental degradation and in economic growth (figure 8f). Degradation includes the costs of greenhouse gas emissions from fossil fuels, agriculture, forestry, and land use change; the harvest of forest timber resources beyond sustainable rates; and reduced labor output due to premature mortality caused by exposure to environmental risk factors such as air pollution, unsafe water and sanitation, and harmful substances in the workplace.[3]

With strong decoupling, environmental degradation declines while the economy continues to grow (green area in figure 8f). However, most countries show weak decoupling or intensified coupling. With weak decoupling, degradation may decline, but at a slower rate than economic growth (blue area in figure 8f). About 80 percent of low-income countries show weak decoupling, owing largely to reduced health risks from household air pollution and unsafe water and sanitation. With intensified coupling, degradation increases at an even faster rate than economic growth (red area in figure 8f). About 40 percent of middle-income countries and 70 percent of high-income countries show intensified coupling.

Degradation per dollar of economic output continues to be nearly 20 times higher in low-income countries than in high-income countries. And illnesses due to exposure to environmental health risks cause more than 9 million premature deaths each year. That is 16 percent of all deaths recorded for 2015, and three times more deaths than were attributed to malaria, HIV and AIDS, and tuberculosis combined.[4] So any analysis of decoupling should also consider the magnitude of degradation and the ability of people and the natural environment to cope with these pressures.

Expanding access to financial services

Financial services enable individuals to manage and enhance their incomes, assets, and investments (target 8.10). Having a transaction account is more useful when there is a broad network of access points with wide geographic coverage.

By the end of 2015 there were 1,214 access points to financial services per 100,000 adults worldwide, up 19 percent from 2014 (figure 8g). Access points can be grouped into four categories: automated teller machines, point-of-sale terminals, branches of payment services providers, and agents of payment services providers.[5]

In 2015 the number of point-of-sale terminals increased by 9 million globally, to 1 per 100 adults. In recent years, the number of automated teller machines has also increased, but at a slower rate than the number of point-of-sale terminals. In addition to traditional services (such as withdrawals, deposits, and account inquiries), the expansion of automated teller machine functions enables customers to perform a broader range of transactions.

Agents—entities that provide some banking and retail payment services on behalf of a payment service provider—have spread across some regions and provide financial services to areas and populations that are underserved

8g Points of access to financial services worldwide grew 19 percent in 2015
Average annual growth rate of access points, per 100,000 adults (%)

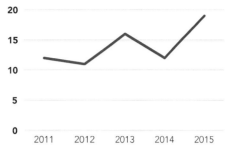

Source: World Bank Global Payment Systems survey.

by traditional bank branches or are otherwise unprofitable. In 2015 more than half a million new payment services provider agents were established in 25 countries where 70 percent of the world's unbanked population resides.

Notes

1. World Bank. 2012. *World Development Report 2013: Jobs*. Washington, DC.

2. P. Falco, A. Kerr, P. Paci, and B. Rijkers. 2014. "Working Toward Better Pay: Earning Dynamics in Ghana and Tanzania." World Bank, Washington, DC.

3. World Bank staff estimates using data on greenhouse gas emissions from CDIAC (Carbon Dioxide Information Analysis Center, Oak Ridge National Laboratory, U.S. Department of Energy), 2015, Fossil-Fuel CO_2 Emissions (http://cdiac.ornl.gov/trends/emis/meth_reg .html) and Food and Agriculture Organization, 2016, FAOSTAT database (http://faostat3.fao .org); data on roundwood harvest and exports from FAO (2016); data on premature mortality due to environment-related health risks from IHME (Institute for Health Metrics and Evaluation), 2016, *Global Burden of Disease Study 2015* (http://ghdx.healthdata.org/gbd-results-tool).

4. See Forouzanfar et al. (2016); data may be accessed at the IHME, Global Health Data Exchange, GBD Results Tool.

5. Some double counting may occur.

Industry, innovation, and infrastructure

9 Build resilient infrastructure, promote inclusive and sustainable industrialization, and foster innovation

Just over half the rural population in Nepal live within 2 kilometers of a road in good or fair condition, leaving around 10.3 million people without easy access. And around 15 million rural residents lack good road access in Mozambique. Yet reliable roads and other decent infrastructure are essential for lifting rural communities out of poverty. Goal 9 explores not only opportunities to improve transport but also those in industry, innovation, and other types of infrastructure.

Promoting industry

Goal 9 promotes inclusive and sustainable industrialization (target 9.2). Manufacturing value added (MVA) is an indicator for assessing a country's industrialization, and MVA's share in gross domestic product (GDP) measures the role of manufacturing in the economy.

Worldwide, MVA as a share of GDP has been declining for more than two decades, from 21 percent in 1995 to 15 percent in 2014, in contrast to the rise in the share of services. It was lowest in Sub-Saharan Africa (11 percent) of regions with data available for 2015. By comparison, it was 16 percent in Europe and Central Asia, 16 percent in South Asia, and 14 percent in Latin America and the Caribbean. MVA per capita shows a similar pattern. It was $3,114 per person in Europe and Central Asia in 2015, $1,123 in Latin America and the Caribbean, and just $144 per person in Sub-Saharan Africa.

Sub-Saharan Africa also had considerable variation among countries (figure 9a). Equatorial Guinea, Mauritius, and Swaziland had the highest MVA per capita at $2,124, $1,209, and $1,188 in 2015, while most countries in the region recorded less than $200.[1]

Supporting rural markets and services

Investment in reliable, sustainable, and resilient infrastructure can provide remote populations with access to services (target 9.1). With better roads, farmers can bring produce to markets more efficiently, and families can more easily get to schools, hospitals, and other facilities. Enhancing rural road connectivity also helps in the long term by elevating agricultural productivity, business profitability, and employment.

The rural access index (RAI) measures the proportion of people within two kilometers of an all-season road—a reasonable walking distance for people's normal economic and social purposes. RAIs are currently available for eight countries in Africa and Asia (figure 9d), integrating population data from censuses, surveys, social media, and administrative systems with satellite and other spatial datasets to produce high-resolution population distribution data. In addition to traditional road assessment surveys, road quality or "road roughness" data are captured through smartphone apps while driving matched with high-resolution satellite imagery.

Around 174 million rural dwellers in the eight countries lack good access to roads, of a total population of more than 461.7 million. Access varies according to population density, degree of urbanization, and level of economic development, and the rural access index ranges from 87 percent in Bangladesh to 17 percent in Zambia (figures 9b and 9c). But due to a much larger population, the number of people without access in Bangladesh (16 million) is more than twice that in Zambia (7 million). Of the eight countries,

9a Manufacturing value added varies considerably in Sub-Saharan Africa

Manufacturing value added, most recent value available for 2014–15

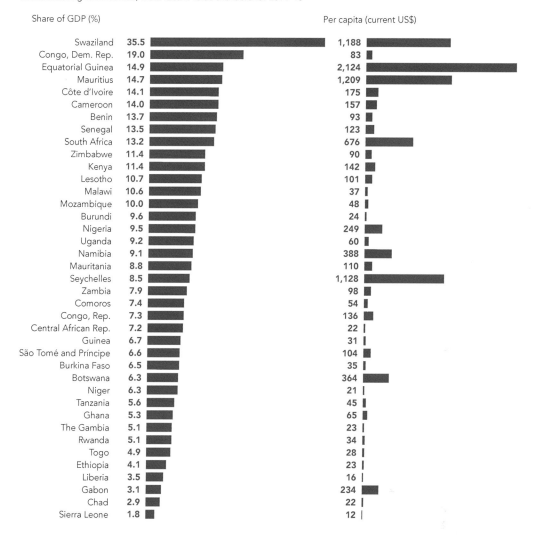

	Share of GDP (%)	Per capita (current US$)
Swaziland	35.5	1,188
Congo, Dem. Rep.	19.0	83
Equatorial Guinea	14.9	2,124
Mauritius	14.7	1,209
Côte d'Ivoire	14.1	175
Cameroon	14.0	157
Benin	13.7	93
Senegal	13.5	123
South Africa	13.2	676
Zimbabwe	11.4	90
Kenya	11.4	142
Lesotho	10.7	101
Malawi	10.6	37
Mozambique	10.0	48
Burundi	9.6	24
Nigeria	9.5	249
Uganda	9.2	60
Namibia	9.1	388
Mauritania	8.8	110
Seychelles	8.5	1,128
Zambia	7.9	98
Comoros	7.4	54
Congo, Rep.	7.3	136
Central African Rep.	7.2	22
Guinea	6.7	31
São Tomé and Príncipe	6.6	104
Burkina Faso	6.5	35
Botswana	6.3	364
Niger	6.3	21
Tanzania	5.6	45
Ghana	5.3	65
The Gambia	5.1	23
Rwanda	5.1	34
Togo	4.9	28
Ethiopia	4.1	23
Liberia	3.5	16
Gabon	3.1	234
Chad	2.9	22
Sierra Leone	1.8	12

Source: World Bank national accounts data; United Nations Population Division; WDI (NV.IND.MANF.ZS, NV.IND.MANF.CD, SP.POP.TOTL).

9b The share of rural dwellers who lack good access to roads can vary widely...

Rural access index (year varies by country)

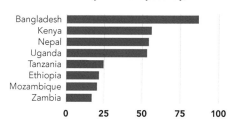

Source: World Bank, 2016, *Measuring rural access: Using new technologies,* Washington, DC.

9c ...but the overall number of rural dwellers cut off from markets is in the millions

Population without access (millions)

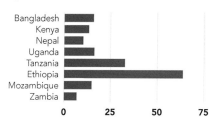

Source: World Bank, 2016, *Measuring rural access: Using new technologies,* Washington, DC.

9d Rural access varied from 17 percent in Zambia to 87 percent in Bangladesh
Rural access index (%)

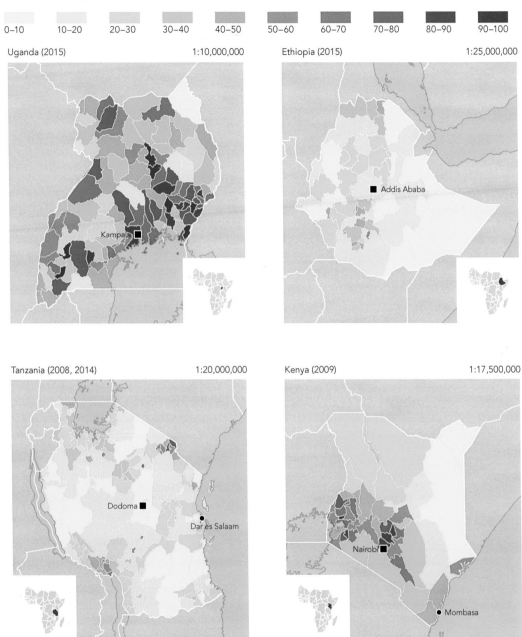

Note: The rural access index is the proportion of people who live within two kilometers of an all-season road.

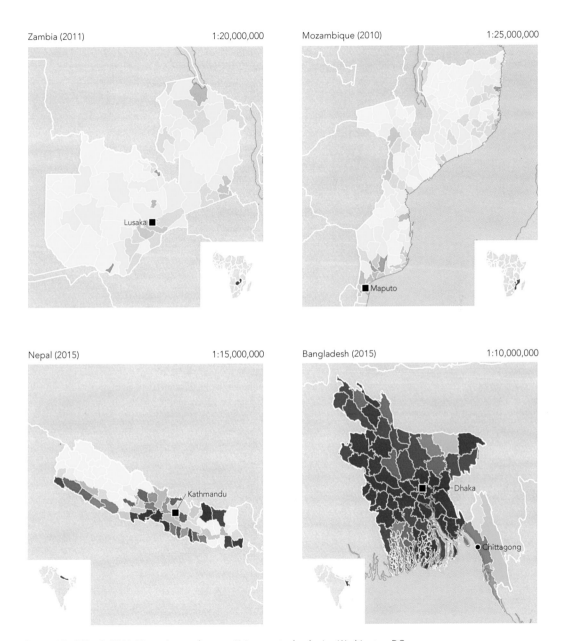

Zambia (2011) 1:20,000,000

Lusaka ■

Mozambique (2010) 1:25,000,000

Maputo

Nepal (2015) 1:15,000,000

Kathmandu

Bangladesh (2015) 1:10,000,000

Dhaka

Chittagong

Source: World Bank, 2016, *Measuring rural access: Using new technologies*, Washington, DC.

9e Air freight has risen by 60 percent over the last 15 years globally
Air freight (billion ton-kilometers)

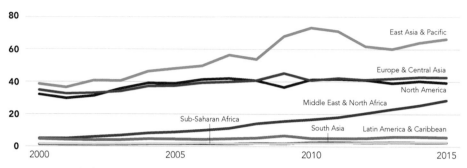

Note: Region in which the carrier is registered.
Source: International Civil Aviation Organization; WDI (IS.AIR.GOOD.MT.K1).

Ethiopia has the most people without access to an all-season road—almost 64 million.

Developing regional and transborder infrastructure

Reliable and frequent air transport is vital to efficient regional and transborder infrastructure (target 9.1). Between 2000 and 2015 global air passenger transport doubled, to reach 3.4 billion passengers, of which 1 billion were in carriers registered in East Asia and Pacific. The region tripled its passenger numbers between 2000 and 2015, a trend which has been driven primarily by China. Carriers registered in North America and in Europe and Central Asia accounted for 26 percent each of the global total.

Air freight rose by almost 60 percent between 2000 and 2015, to reach 188 billion ton-km globally (figure 9e). The share of global freight transported by carriers registered in the Middle East and North Africa increased rapidly from 4 percent in 2000 to 15 percent in 2015. The trend has been primarily driven by the United Arab Emirates and Qatar.

Improving resource-use efficiency

Goal 9 seeks to improve resource-use efficiency and promote greater adoption of clean and environmentally sound technologies and industrial processes (target 9.4). Carbon dioxide (CO_2) emissions per unit of GDP captures

efficiency in both energy production and consumption, along with use of fuels and clean technologies.

Global CO_2 emissions per unit of GDP declined by about one quarter during the last two decades. Only the Middle East and North Africa showed a slight increase during this period. East Asia and Pacific has the highest carbon intensity of GDP, despite a 13 percent decline between 1990 and 2013 The carbon intensity of GDP fell by 38 percent in North America and by 42 percent in Europe and Central Asia over the same period.[2]

Encouraging innovation

Investing in research and development (R&D) across sectors and facilitating innovation in science and technology are two ways that Goal 9 hopes to raise the competitiveness of developing countries (target 9.5). R&D expenditure as a share of GDP and the proportion of people working in R&D tend to be highest in high-income economies. Japan invested nearly 4 percent of GDP in R&D in 2014, higher than the shares invested in recent years by Singapore, the United States, and other upper-middle-income economies including China, Russia, and Malaysia (figure 9f). Japan recorded nearly 2,600 patent applications per million people in 2014, the highest of any country, indicative of its supportive environment for innovation.

9f Japan, the United States, and Singapore invest heavily in research and development

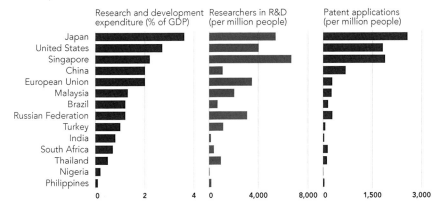

Source: UNESCO; World Intellectual Property Organization; United Nations Population Division; WDI (GB. XPD.RSDV.GD.ZS, SP.POP.SCIE.RD.P6, IP.PAT.NRES, IP.PAT.RESD, SP.POP.TOTL). Most recent data available for 2010–14, and 2007 R&D data for Nigeria.

9g Many small and medium-size enterprises lack financing
Small and medium-size enterprises with a loan or line of credit (%)

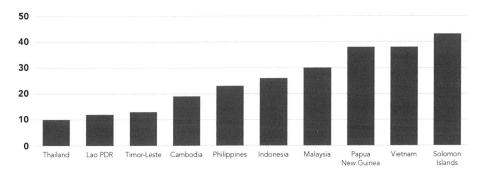

Source: Enterprise Surveys (database), World Bank, Washington, DC. http://www.enterprisesurveys.org.

Financing small and medium-size enterprises

Access to financial services enables firms to smooth cash flows, accumulate assets, make productive investments, and promote better use of resources (target 9.3). Yet many small enterprises around the world, formal or informal, lack the financing they need. Enterprise surveys[3] in East Asia and Pacific during 2015 and 2016 showed that, in the 10 economies surveyed, small and medium-size enterprises are credit-constrained (figure 9g). In Thailand only one in ten SMEs has a loan or line of credit, and in Vietnam fewer than one in four SMEs.

Notes

1. Data for Swaziland are for 2014.

2. Data for Europe and Central Asia cover the period 1992–2013.

3. World Bank Enterprise Surveys have been collecting firm-level data (representative of an economy's private sector) in more than 130 economies around the world for over 10 years. Surveys are implemented every year in around 20 countries.

(≡) Reduced inequalities

10 Reduce inequality within and among countries

The income and consumption of the poorest 40 percent of the population (the "bottom 40") grew faster than the national average in 49 of 83 countries between 2008 and 2013. By providing a platform for sustained income growth among the poorer segments of society, Goal 10 aims to reduce inequalities between a country's citizens and to promote shared prosperity and gains in wealth for all.

While the growth of the poorest 40 percent outpaced the national average in more than half the countries with data, it was negative in eight countries. Most were high-income countries, among them Iceland, the Netherlands, Portugal, the United Kingdom, and the United States (see figure 10c on page 58, left).

By contrast, in 34 of the 83 countries with data, per capita income or consumption of the bottom 40 grew slower than the national average from 2008 to 2013. In 15 of the 34 the income or consumption of the bottom 40 contracted. In most of these 15 countries (such as Greece and Serbia), living conditions deteriorated overall but even more quickly among the poorest (see figure 10c on page 59, right).

To reduce inequality and promote shared prosperity, Goal 10 looks to achieve sustained income growth among the poorest 40 percent of the population (the bottom 40) at a rate higher than the national average (target 10.1).

The World Bank's Global Database of Shared Prosperity covers 83 countries, with 75 percent of the world's people, with most recent estimates available for 2013. In the Middle East and North Africa only 2 of 20 countries have sufficient data for estimating shared prosperity indicators. Estimates are available for 8 of 29 countries in East Asia and Pacific and for 9 of 48 countries in Sub-Saharan Africa (figure 10a).

Reducing the costs of migration

Goal 10 also seeks to address inequality by facilitating orderly, safe, regular, and responsible migration and mobility of people (target 10.7).

As advanced economies demand more nontradable services, the need for low-skilled labor in

10a The geographical coverage of shared prosperity data is uneven across regions
Shared prosperity data availability (number of countries)

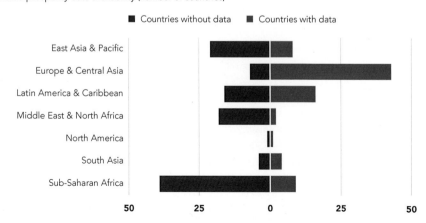

Source: World Bank Global Database of Shared Prosperity; WDI (SI.SPR.PC40.ZG, SI.SPR.PCAP.ZG).

10b Recruitment costs are often higher than one month's earnings

Recruitment costs (months of earnings at destination)

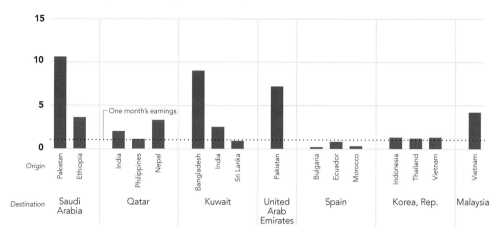

Note: All surveyed Sri Lankan workers in Kuwait were females engaged in domestic help services.
Source: KNOMAD survey data of migrant workers.

construction, caregiving, and domestic help has been rising. Although transport costs declined in the 20th century, the costs of moving between countries remain high.[1] This is especially pertinent for the low skilled, who, unlike the high skilled, tend to pay their initial recruitment costs out of pocket, which can amount to several years of earnings in home countries. These high costs inhibit global mobility of the low skilled, especially the financially constrained poor, and reduce potential remittances.

Recruitment costs can be grouped in three major categories: costs to comply with laws and regulations of origin and destination countries (such as obtaining work permits or medical check-ups), fees paid to recruitment agents, and internal and international transportation costs.

Those costs vary considerably across migration corridors.[2] For workers from various countries of origin going to Spain and Korea, and workers from the Philippines going to Qatar, they amount to about one month's earnings (or about 8 percent of annual earnings). But for workers from Pakistan in low-skilled jobs in Saudi Arabia, the recruitment costs are about 11 months' earnings (or about $4,400 in 2014 dollars), and for those from Ethiopia about 4 months' earnings (or close to $1,000 in 2014 dollars) (figure 10b).

Lowering remittance transaction costs

In addition to recruitment costs, many migrants incur costs sending money home. Remittances totaled an estimated $582 billion in 2015, sent by about 232 million migrants. Of this, $432 billion went to low- and middle-income countries.[3]

The costs of remitting money can be very high relative to the amount sent and relative to the low incomes of migrant workers and their families in the home country. Goal 10 calls for reducing the transaction costs of migrant remittances to less than 3 percent and for eliminating remittance corridors with costs higher than 5 percent (target 10.c). This target includes the G20 commitment to reduce the global average to 5 percent.

At an average cost of 15 percent of the total sent, for those countries with available data, South Africa was the most costly G20 country to send money from in 2015; at 2 percent Russia is the least costly (figure 10d). Among remittance-receiving G20 countries, China is the most expensive to send money to, at 10 percent of the total sent, and Mexico the cheapest, at 6 percent (figure 10e).

Moreover, sending money through post offices and money transfer operators (at a little over 6 percent) is cheaper than going through a

10c In 6 of 10 countries with data the per capita income or consumption of the bottom 40 grew faster than the national average between 2008 and 2013

Annualized per capita growth rate, 2008–13 (%)

Where incomes of the poorest people are growing faster than average

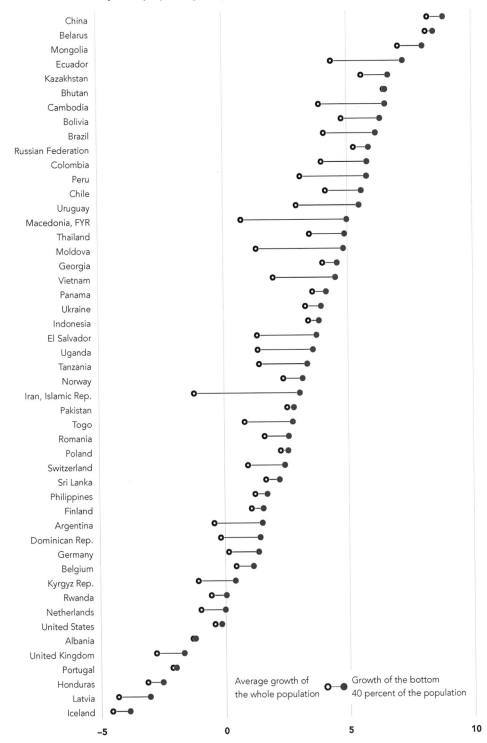

Source: World Bank Global Database of Shared Prosperity; WDI (SI.SPR.PC40.ZG, SI.SPR.PCAP.ZG).

Annualized per capita growth rate, 2008–13 (%)

Where incomes of the poorest people are growing slower than average

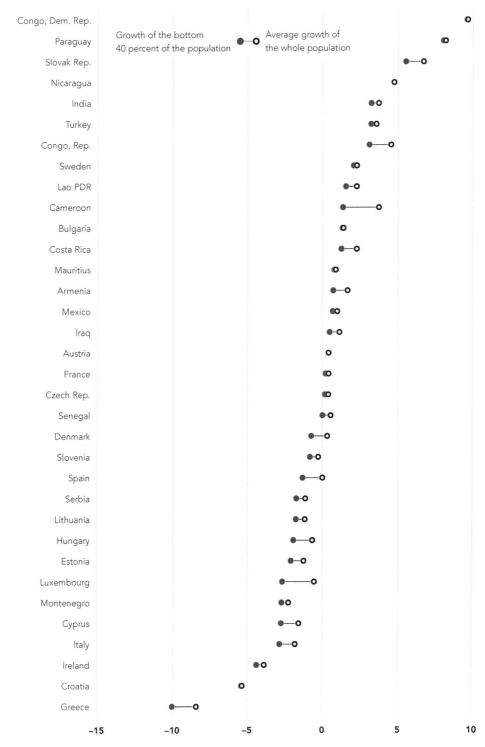

10d Among G20 countries with data, South Africa is the costliest to send remittances from
Average cost of sending the equivalent of $200 in remittances from G20 countries, 2015 (%)

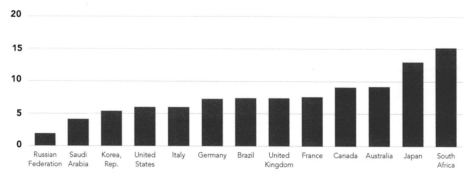

Note: Data available for 13 G20 countries.
Source: World Bank Remittance Prices Worldwide database (http://remittanceprices.worldbank.org/en); WDI (SI.RMT.COST.OB.ZS).

10e Among G20 countries with data, China is the costliest to send remittances to
Average cost of sending the equivalent of $200 in remittances to G20 countries, 2015 (%)

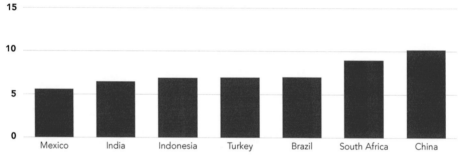

Note: Data available for 7 G20 countries.
Source: World Bank Remittance Prices Worldwide database (http://remittanceprices.worldbank.org/en); WDI (SI.RMT.COST.IB.ZS).

commercial bank (at 11 percent). With new and improved technologies, prepaid cards and mobile operators have become the cheapest ways of sending money home, reducing the cost to 2 to 4 percent.

Elsewhere, in non-G20 countries remittance costs can remain high for receiving countries —such as in Sub-Saharan Africa (on average 10 percent), a large outlay for a region where many families rely heavily on overseas remittances.

In the 22 countries where total personal remittances received were more than 10 percent of GDP in 2015, the cost varies greatly (figure 10f). It is less than 3 percent of the total in Armenia, Georgia, Kyrgyz Republic, and Tajikistan, where the majority of the remittances originate from Russia—one of the least expensive countries for

remitting money. In the remaining 18 countries, costs are much higher, well above the 3 percent target. In 2015 it was most expensive to send remittances to Lebanon at 13 percent, and 16 percent of Lebanon's GDP came from personal remittances. In Nepal the top recipient country in remittances as a share of GDP, the cost is 4 percent.

Changing the focus of aid delivery

Goal 10 encourages the flow of aid to where the need is greatest (target 10.b). Since 2010, 70 percent of bilateral aid has been channeled directly to recipient countries by donors, and the remaining 30 percent through multilateral institutions. But a marked change in its composition reflects the increasing demands of humanitarian crises and, more recently, the surge in refugees and migrants into European countries that belong to

10f The average cost of sending remittances to top receiving countries remains very high

Average cost of sending the equivalent of $200 in remittances, by receiving countries, 2015 (%)

Personal remittances received, 2015 (% of GDP)

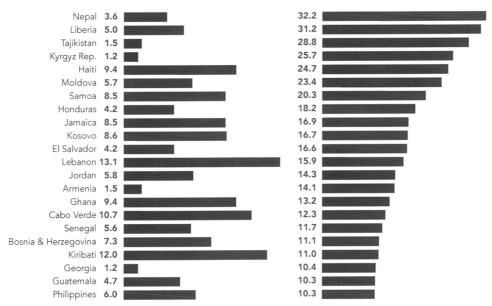

Country	Cost		Remittances
Nepal	3.6		32.2
Liberia	5.0		31.2
Tajikistan	1.5		28.8
Kyrgyz Rep.	1.2		25.7
Haiti	9.4		24.7
Moldova	5.7		23.4
Samoa	8.5		20.3
Honduras	4.2		18.2
Jamaica	8.5		16.9
Kosovo	8.6		16.7
El Salvador	4.2		16.6
Lebanon	13.1		15.9
Jordan	5.8		14.3
Armenia	1.5		14.1
Ghana	9.4		13.2
Cabo Verde	10.7		12.3
Senegal	5.6		11.7
Bosnia & Herzegovina	7.3		11.1
Kiribati	12.0		11.0
Georgia	1.2		10.4
Guatemala	4.7		10.3
Philippines	6.0		10.3

Note: Data are the annual average for remittances receiving countries. Data on the cost of sending remittances for Kiribati are for 2011.
Source: World Bank Remittance Prices Worldwide database (http://remittanceprices.worldbank.org/en); WDI (SI.RMT.COST.ZS, BX.TRF.PWKR.DT.GD.ZS).

the Organisation for Economic Co-operation and Development Development Assistance Committee. Humanitarian and food aid and in-donor country expenditure on refugees, taken together, doubled in volume between 2010 and 2015, and their combined share of all net bilateral aid rose from about 16 percent to 28 percent (figure 10g).

This upward trend in in–donor country refugee costs contrasts with an observed slowdown in net bilateral aid for development projects and programs, including technical cooperation. In 2015 the latter rose only by an estimated 1.8 percent in real terms.

Notes

1. Flanagan, Robert J. 2006. *Globalization and Labor Conditions: Working Conditions and Worker Rights in a Global Economy.* New York: Oxford University Press.

2. To better understand the magnitude and structure of migration costs, the World Bank's KNOMAD (Global Knowledge Partnership on Migration and Development) has compiled a novel

10g Shares of in–donor country refugee costs and humanitarian and food aid have increased significantly since 2010
Distribution of net bilateral aid flows (%)

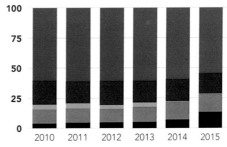

- Bilateral development projects and programs
- Technical cooperation
- Debt relief
- Humanitarian and food aid
- In–donor country refugee costs

Source: OECD–DAC.

dataset on migration costs incurred by low-skilled migrants, in collaboration with the ILO. The dataset is based on interviewing migrants who went to foreign jobs mostly through a regular channel.

3. World Bank Remittance Prices Worldwide database.

▟▙ Sustainable cities and communities

11 Make cities and human settlements inclusive, safe, resilient, and sustainable

The number of urban dwellers is growing by 2 percent a year globally, but by 4 percent in Sub-Saharan Africa, which will double the number of people in the region's cities in two decades. Cities are engines of economic growth and offer opportunities for innovation and sustainable development. But Goal 11 recognizes that urban areas still face numerous challenges in ensuring access for all to safe housing, affordable transport, clean air, and green and public spaces.

Ensuring access to safe and adequate housing

Achieving Goal 11 requires providing access for all to basic services and to adequate, safe, and affordable housing (target 11.1). For many cities this means improving and upgrading slum areas, where many of the poor live. According to the United Nations Human Settlements Programme (UN-HABITAT), slums are areas where households lack durable housing, sufficient living space, secure tenure, or easy access to safe water or adequate sanitation facilities.

Countries have made considerable progress in recent years, but the percentage of urban populations living in slums[1] remains very high. In Sub-Saharan Africa an average of 67 percent of the urban population was living in slum conditions in 1990; by 2014 this had fallen to 55 percent (figure 11a). But the last decade saw rises in several countries. Between 2005 and 2014, slum populations in Burkina Faso rose by 6 percentage points, in Lesotho by nearly 16 percentage points, and in Zimbabwe by 7 percentage points.

Improving air quality in cities

As rural residents move to cities in search of better livelihoods, reducing the adverse impact on the environment is crucial to building safer and more sustainable cities (target 11.6). Air quality and waste management are two areas of environmental impact needing urgent attention.

11a More than half of all urban dwellers in Sub-Saharan Africa live in slums
Share of urban population living in slums, 2014 (%)

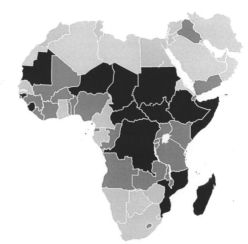

Source: UN-HABITAT; WDI (EN.POP.SLUM.UR.ZS).

Air quality is commonly measured by levels of $PM_{2.5}$: particulate matter less than or equal to 2.5 microns in diameter. The World Health Organization recommends that $PM_{2.5}$ levels not exceed 10 micrograms per cubic meter as a guideline for average annual $PM_{2.5}$. Long-term exposure to pollution above this level has been shown to increase the risk of fatal illness. It is estimated that nearly 92 percent of the world's people live in places where this safe level is exceeded.[2] In three regions levels of mean annual exposure have worsened since 1990,

11b The highest levels of air pollution are in the Middle East

PM$_{2.5}$ air pollution, mean annual exposure, 2015 (micrograms per cubic meter) 49 highest countries.

Qatar
Saudi Arabia
Egypt, Arab Rep.
Bangladesh
Mauritania
Libya
Nepal
India
Kuwait
Cameroon
Pakistan
United Arab Emirates
Niger
The Gambia
Uganda
China
Bhutan
Bahrain
Myanmar
Oman
Congo, Rep.
Yemen, Rep.
Iraq
Djibouti
Sudan
Tajikistan
Rwanda
Afghanistan
Bosnia & Herzegovina
Equatorial Guinea
Central African Rep.
Congo, Dem. Rep.
Chad
Burundi
Tunisia
Mali
World
Eritrea
Iran, Islamic Rep.
Syrian Arab Rep.
Macedonia, FYR
Burkina Faso
Gabon
Uzbekistan
Cabo Verde
Jordan
Nigeria
Honduras
Senegal
El Salvador

1990 ○—● 2015

0   50   100   150

Source: Institute for Health Metrics and Evaluation, University of Washington, Seattle, WA; WDI (EN. ATM.PM25.MC.M3).

and the global level increased from 39.6 micrograms per cubic meter in 1990 to 44 in 2015. Of the 194 countries with data in 2015, only 26 reported safe levels of PM$_{2.5}$, and in 145 countries more than 99 percent of the population was exposed to unsafe levels. In Egypt, Qatar, and Saudi Arabia, the PM$_{2.5}$ levels are 10 times the recommended level—more than 100 micrograms per cubic meter (figure 11b).

Defining "urban"

The terms "urban" and "rural" are often used to understand how environments and the lives of those within them differ around the world. But there is no consistent international definition of "urban." Instead, each country has its own classifications to identify its urban population, and these vary widely across countries. Criteria include combinations of population size, population density, type of economic activity, physical characteristics, and level of infrastructure.

11c "Urban" areas range from 200 to 50,000 habitants

Minimum population threshold considered "urban" (number of countries)

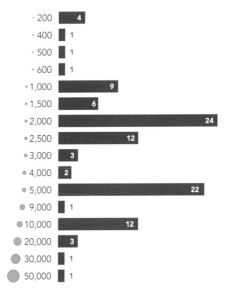

Threshold	Countries
· 200	4
· 400	1
· 500	1
· 600	1
· 1,000	9
· 1,500	6
· 2,000	24
· 2,500	12
· 3,000	3
· 4,000	2
· 5,000	22
· 9,000	1
· 10,000	12
· 20,000	3
· 30,000	1
· 50,000	1

Note: Circles show relative population sizes.
Source: World Urbanization Prospects: The 2014 Revision (database), United Nations, Department of Economic and Social Affairs, New York, https://esa.un.org/unpd/wup/.

11d In some countries, slum dwellers make up a large share of the urban population
2014 (percent)

- Urban population living in slums
- Urban population living outside slums
- Rural population

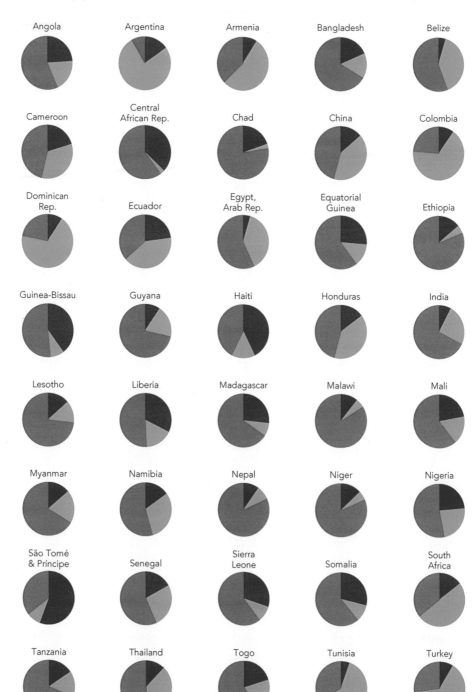

Angola	Argentina	Armenia	Bangladesh	Belize
Cameroon	Central African Rep.	Chad	China	Colombia
Dominican Rep.	Ecuador	Egypt, Arab Rep.	Equatorial Guinea	Ethiopia
Guinea-Bissau	Guyana	Haiti	Honduras	India
Lesotho	Liberia	Madagascar	Malawi	Mali
Myanmar	Namibia	Nepal	Niger	Nigeria
São Tomé & Príncipe	Senegal	Sierra Leone	Somalia	South Africa
Tanzania	Thailand	Togo	Tunisia	Turkey

Benin	Brazil	Burkina Faso	Burundi	Cambodia
Comoros	Congo, Dem. Rep.	Congo, Rep.	Costa Rica	Côte d'Ivoire
Gabon	The Gambia	Ghana	Guatemala	Guinea
Indonesia	Iraq	Jordan	Kenya	Lao PDR
Mauritania	Mexico	Mongolia	Morocco	Mozambique
Pakistan	Panama	Peru	Philippines	Rwanda
South Sudan	Sudan	Suriname	Swaziland	Syrian Arab Rep.
Uganda	Vietnam	Yemen, Rep.	Zambia	Zimbabwe

Source: United Nations, World Urbanization Prospects; UN-HABITAT; WDI (EN.POP.SLUM.UR.ZS, SP.RUR.TOTL), (SP.URB.TOTL).

11e Regional urbanization varies dramatically depending on the approach
Proportion of population in high-density and urban clusters, using European Commission approach (%)

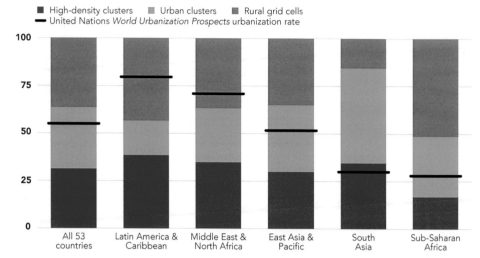

Source: C. Deuskar and B. Stewart, 2016, "Measuring Global Urbanization Using a Standard Definition of Urban Areas: Analysis of Preliminary Results," paper presented at the World Bank Land and Poverty Conference 2016, Washington, DC, March 3–4; WDI (SP.URB.TOTL.IN.ZS).

About 100 countries use some form of minimum population threshold to define a settlement as "urban." These thresholds range from as few as 200 people to as many as 50,000. The average minimum population threshold is just under 5,000 inhabitants (figure 11c).

This inconsistency is like comparing apples and oranges, where a city of 1,000 is urban in one country, while a city of 10,000 is rural in another. These conflicting definitions make it difficult to make meaningful cross-country comparisons, let alone establish consistent estimates of urbanization worldwide.

The European Commission (EC) has developed an approach to standardize the definition of urban areas by using population distribution grids consisting of one square kilometer cells. "High density" clusters of grid cells are those with 1,500 inhabitants per square kilometers and a minimum combined population of 50,000. "Urban" clusters have 300 inhabitants per square kilometers and a minimum combined population of 5,000, while "rural" clusters make up all remaining grid cells.

Gridded population distribution data are available from WorldPop[3] and Global Human Settlements Population Layer (GHS Pop).[4] Analyzing these datasets using the EC clustering approach results in higher estimates of urban population (64 percent on average) for the 80 countries in the analysis, relative to estimates from the United Nations World Urbanization Prospects,[5] which relies on national definitions of urbanization (57 percent on average).

The distribution of urban populations across regions varies dramatically depending on the approach. Using the EC clustering approach, countries in Asia and Africa appear to be more urbanized than their national definitions of "urban" would suggest, whereas the opposite is true for countries in Latin America (figure 11e).

As satellite data continue to become available at higher frequencies and resolutions, we draw closer to standardizing the way urbanization is defined and measured globally. The German space agency DLR recently released a global map of built-up areas derived from radar data (Global Urban Footprint),[6] and the European Space Agency's Urban Thematic Exploitation Program[7] allows nontechnical users to customize results through supercomputing power and tools. These advances herald a new frontier in understanding urbanization worldwide.

Notes

1. The proportion of people living in slums is measured by a proxy, represented by the urban population living in households with at least one of four characteristics: lack of access to an improved water supply; lack of access to improved sanitation facilities; overcrowding (three or more persons per room); and dwellings made of non-durable material.

2. See WDI indicator *PM$_{2.5}$ air pollution, population exposed to levels exceeding WHO guideline value (% of total)* (EN.ATM.PM25.MC.ZS). Data are as of February 1, 2017.

3. http://www.worldpop.org.uk/.

4. http://ghsl.jrc.ec.europa.eu/.

5. https://esa.un.org/unpd/wup/.

6. http://www.dlr.de/.

7. https://urban-tep.eo.esa.int.

∞ Responsible consumption and production

12 Ensure sustainable consumption and production patterns

The equivalent of more than 500 kilocalories of food per person a day is lost in the supply chain in Latin America and the Caribbean before it even gets to the final consumer. By reducing such waste, and promoting recycling, reuse, and more efficient practices across high-consumption economies and those highly dependent on natural resources, Goal 12 looks to bolster the mechanisms for sustainable development to flourish.

Doing more with less

Goal 12 aims at "doing more and better with less," increasing net welfare gains from economic activities by reducing resource use, degradation, and pollution. It involves different stakeholders across the full production cycle, including business, consumers, policymakers, media, and communities. It addresses aspects ranging from resource and chemical use to food loss, solid waste, recycling, consumer behavior, subsidies, technology, tourism, and government procurement.

Balancing the use of natural resources to foster growth

Goal 12 encourages the efficient use and sustainable management of natural resources (target 12.2). The difference between national production and consumption—the policy-induced change in a country's wealth—is measured by adjusted net savings. This takes into account investment in human capital, depreciation of fixed capital, depletion of natural resources, and pollution damage. Consistently negative saving rates indicate diminishing wealth and unsustainable development. Positive savings form the basis for future growth.

Resource-rich countries that depend heavily on extractive industries ideally balance the depletion of their natural resources by investing in other forms of capital, such as building human capital through education.

A comparison of average saving rates to the average share of natural resource rents in national income over 1990 to 2014 reveals that many low-income countries are undercutting the productive base of their economies over the longer term (see figure 12c on page 70). Adjusted net savings in low-income countries averaged -0.4 percent of gross national income (GNI), meaning their national savings and investment in human capital are less than their capital depletion. In contrast, it averaged +13.7 percent of GNI in the lower-middle-income countries, +15.6 percent in upper-middle-income countries, and +8.6 percent in high-income countries.

Forgoing some consumption by increasing savings and reinvestment of resource rents is a tough proposition in poorer countries, where living standards are already low. But improving the sustainable and efficient management of resources in these countries will be critical for long-term growth and development.

Minimizing food loss and waste

Food loss can occur at any stage of the food supply chain, and refers to decreases in both food quantity and food quality. Goal 12 seeks to minimize waste throughout the chain (target 12.3). Food loss estimates are based on FAO food balance sheets that do not, however, include post-consumer food waste. Per capita food losses have risen in most regions since

1995 and are now highest in Latin American and the Caribbean, where they averaged 521 kilocalories per capita a day in 2011, up from 329 in 1995 (figure 12a). North America dropped considerably from 190 kilocalories per capita a day in 1995 to the lowest of all regions (71 kilocalories per capita per day) in 2011. Food waste by consumers may account for 28 percent of total food loss in the high-income countries and 7 percent in low- and middle-income countries.[1]

Since 1995 food loss has risen in nearly all categories of food. Fruits and vegetables, and dairy and eggs were lost in 2011 at a rate nearly 50 percent higher than 16 years previously. Only meat, offal, and animals fats fell, with losses in 2011 amounting to around half that lost before reaching consumers in 1995 (figure 12b).

To provide a more complete and accurate picture of global food loss, the Food Loss and Waste Accounting and Reporting Standard was announced at the Global Green Growth Forum in Copenhagen in June 2016.[2] It provides a flexible measurement tool to allow governments, institutions, and agricultural producers and companies to consistently and credibly measure, report on, and manage food loss and waste. Users can identify both food types and inedible parts, and the end destination of

those parts—such as food consumed, animal feed, composting, landfill, refuse, or sewer. A suite of quantification methods under the standard gives users a range of technologies and resources to assess food loss on a comparable basis.

12a Globally, food loss has increased since 1995
Kilocalories per person per day

Source: World Bank staff estimates using FAOSTAT (database), Food and Agriculture Organization.

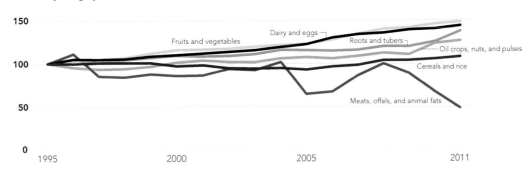

12b Food loss has increased for nearly all types of food, except meat
Food loss by category (index, 1995 = 100)

Source: World Bank staff estimates using FAOSTAT (database), Food and Agriculture Organization.

12c Many resource-dependent countries have negative adjusted net savings

Average adjusted net savings as a share of GNI, 1990–2014 (%)

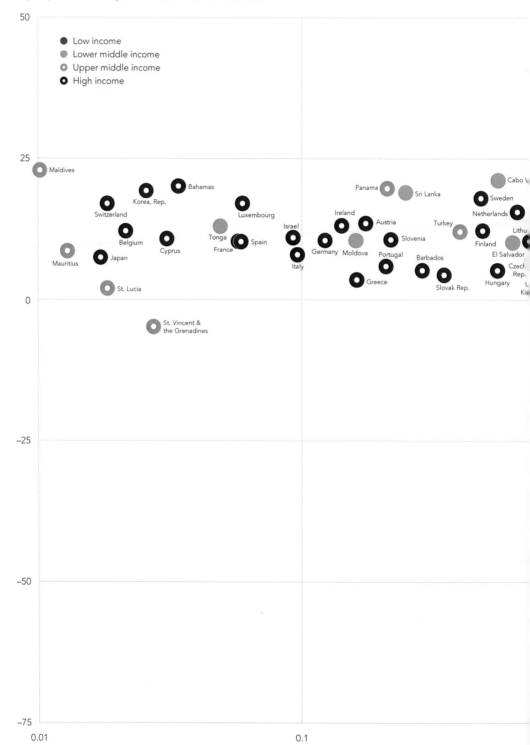

Average natural resource rents as a share of GNI, 1990–2014 (%)

Note: Adjusted net savings is net national savings plus education spending and minus energy, mineral, and forest depletion, carbon dioxide damage, and particulate emission damage.
Source: Preliminary estimates, WDI.

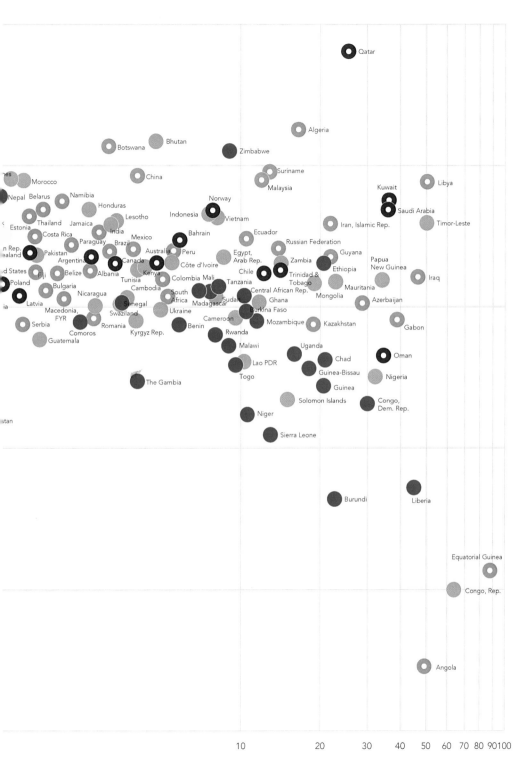

Qatar

Algeria

Bhutan

Botswana

Zimbabwe

Suriname

China

Libya

Malaysia

Kuwait

Norway

Namibia

Morocco

Nepal Belarus

Honduras

Saudi Arabia

Thailand Jamaica

Lesotho

Indonesia

Vietnam

Iran, Islamic Rep.

Timor-Leste

Estonia

India

Costa Rica

Bahrain

Ecuador

Paraguay

Mexico

Russian Federation

n Rep.

ealand

Brazil

Australia

Peru

Pakistan

Côte d'Ivoire

Egypt,
Arab Rep.

Zambia

Guyana

Papua
New Guinea

Argentina

Canada

Chile

Ethiopia

d States

Kenya

Poland

Fiji

Belize

Albania

Tunisia

Colombia Mali

Trinidad &
Tobago

Iraq

Bulgaria

Cambodia

Tanzania

Mauritania

Latvia

Nicaragua

South
Africa

Madagascar

Sudan

Central African Rep.

Ghana

Mongolia

Azerbaijan

ia

Macedonia,
FYR

Senegal

Ukraine

Burkina Faso

Serbia

Swaziland

Cameroon

Mozambique

Kazakhstan

Gabon

Comoros

Romania

Benin

Guatemala

Kyrgyz Rep.

Rwanda

Malawi

Uganda

Chad

Oman

Lao PDR

Guinea-Bissau

Nigeria

The Gambia

Togo

Guinea

stan

Niger

Solomon Islands

Congo,
Dem. Rep.

Sierra Leone

Burundi

Liberia

Equatorial Guinea

Congo, Rep.

Angola

10   20   30   40 50 60 70 80 90100

Average natural resource rents as a share of GNI, 1990–2014 (%)

Recycling and reusing waste

Goal 12 calls on nations to substantially reduce waste through prevention, reduction, recycling, and reuse (target 12.5). Many high-income countries recycle at least a fifth of their municipal solid waste, which is most commonly recorded at the point of final disposal, for example, by weighing trash trucks when they arrive at landfill sites (figure 12d). In low- and middle-income countries, most recycling is through the informal sector and through waste picking, so accurate data are hard to collect, and the contribution of this sector to waste reuse may be underestimated. The International Labour Organization (ILO) estimates that as many as 15 to 20 million people in these countries earn their living from informal recycling activities.[3] And it is estimated that informal waste pickers in India collect and recycle about 60 percent of the 5.6 million tons of plastic waste that the country generates each year.[4]

Adopting sustainable practices

Reporting on sustainability measures has emerged as common practice among many of the world's largest companies. Goal 12 encourages such reporting and the integration of good sustainable processes in all industries and sectors (target 12.6). More than 80 percent of the S&P 500 companies reported on sustainability in 2015, up from just 20 percent in 2011 (figure 12e).[5] Globally, about 73 percent of the largest 100 companies in 45 countries surveyed by KPMG (4,500 companies) report information on corporate responsibility. Three-quarters of these companies reference established guidelines for sustainability reporting by the Global Reporting Initiative, but fewer than half have their corporate responsibility information independently verified and assured by a third party.[6] The growth in sustainability reporting by industry leaders reflects a growing demand by investors and governments for greater disclosure.

12d Singapore has the highest recycling rate of 60 percent, but data are lacking for many countries

Municipal solid waste recycling rates (percent of total waste generated)

0–3   3–20   20–100   No data

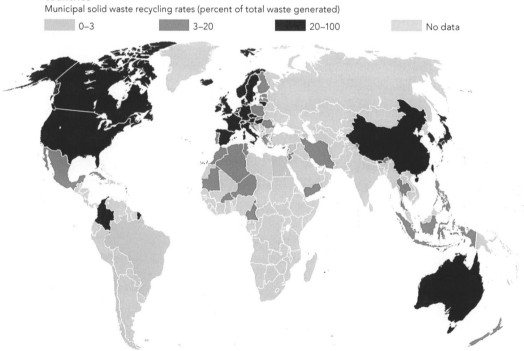

Source: Waste Atlas (database), D-Waste, Athens, http://www.atlas.d-waste.com/.

12e The majority of large companies report on sustainability measures
Share of companies reporting on sustainability measures (%)

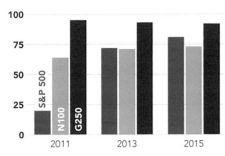

Note: "S&P 500" = Standard & Poor's 500; "N100" = 100 largest companies in 45 countries (4,500 companies total), surveyed by KPMG; "G250" = world's 250 largest companies, according to the Fortune Global 500 rankings in 2014.
Source: Standard & Poor's; KPMG; *Fortune.*

In 2016 governments in more than 50 countries had regulations, guidance, standards, or other policies to encourage or require sustainability reporting by companies and other organizations.[7]

Notes

1. B. Lipinski, C. Hanson, J. Lomax, L. Kitinoja, R. Waite, and T. Searchinger. 2013. "Reducing Food Loss and Waste." Working Paper, World Resources Institute, Washington, DC.

2. World Resources Institute. 2016. *Food Loss and Waste Accounting and Reporting Standard.* Washington, DC. http://www.wri.org/sites/default /files/FLW_Standard_Exec_Summary_final_2016 .pdf.

3. Cited in P. Bhada-Tata and D. Hoornweg. 2015. "Solid Waste and Climate Change." In *State of the World: Can a City Be Sustainable?*, edited by L. Mastny, p. 249. Washington, DC: Island Press.

4. S. Singh. 2013. "India Reports Plastic Waste and Recycling Statistics." *Plastics News,* May 1. http://www.plasticsnews.com/article/20130501 /NEWS/130509998/india-reports-plastic-waste -and-recycling-statistics.

5. Governance & Accountability Institute. 2016. "Flash Report: Eighty One Percent (81%) of the S&P 500 Index Companies Published Corporate Sustainability Reports in 2015." http://www.ga-institute.com/nc/issue-master -system/news-details/article/flash-report-eighty -one-percent-81-of-the-sp-500-index-companies -published-corporate-sustainabi.html.

6. KPMG. 2015. *Currents of Change: The KPMG Survey of Corporate Responsibility Reporting 2015.* Amsterdam: KPMG. http://www.kpmg.com /crreporting.

7. KPMG, Global Reporting Initiative, United Nations Environment Programme, and University of Stellenbosch Business School Centre for Corporate Governance in Africa. 2016. *Carrots & Sticks: Global Trends in Sustainability Reporting Regulation and Policy.* Amsterdam: KPMG. http://www.sseinitiative.org/wp-content /uploads/2016/05/Carrots-Sticks-2016.pdf.

● Climate action

13 Take urgent action to combat climate change and its impacts[1]

Without climate-informed development, climate change could erode development gains and force 100 million more people into extreme poverty by 2030. Climate change is already affecting every country on every continent through changing seasons and weather patterns, rising sea levels, and more extreme weather events. Goal 13 addresses the changes in climate that pose substantial risks for agriculture, water supplies, food production, ecosystems, energy security, and infrastructure.

Understanding the impacts of climate change

Global emissions of carbon dioxide, a major greenhouse gas (GHG) and driver of climate change, increased from 22.4 billion metric tons in 1990 to 35.8 billion in 2013, a rise of 60 percent (figure 13a). The increase in CO_2 emissions and other greenhouse gases has contributed to a rise of about 0.8 degrees Celsius in mean global temperature above preindustrial times.

Continuing emissions of greenhouse gases will cause further warming and changes in all parts of the climate system.[2] Climate change projections use scenarios that approximate levels of GHG buildup (translated as radiative forcing) in the atmosphere. In the lowest-emission scenario, models project a likely mean increase in

global temperature of 1.0°C (±0.7°C) by 2100, relative to 1986–2005. The high-emission scenario models project a likely mean global temperature increase of 3.7°C (±1.1°C), with substantial regional variation under any scenario (figure 13d). Projected changes in annual precipitation also vary greatly depending on the scenario used (figure 13e). Extreme precipitation events over most of the mid-latitude land masses and wet tropical regions are likely to become more intense and more frequent by the end of the century. But under the high-emission scenario, mean annual precipitation is likely to decrease in many mid-latitude and subtropical dry regions.[3]

Given the lag between emissions reduction policies and their impact on global temperatures, an additional warming of at least 1 degree Celsius in the near future is

13a CO_2 emissions are unprecedented
Billions of metric tons

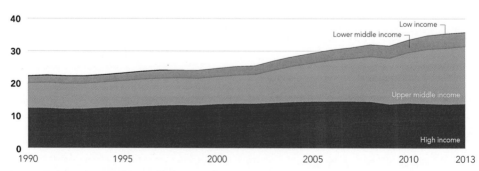

Source: Fossil-Fuel CO_2 Emissions (database), Carbon Dioxide Information Analysis Center, Oak Ridge National Laboratory, Oak Ridge, TN; WDI (EN.ATM.CO2E.KT).

13b Climate change could raise extreme poverty rates substantially by 2030
Percentage point increase in poverty rate

0–1   1–5   5–10   No data

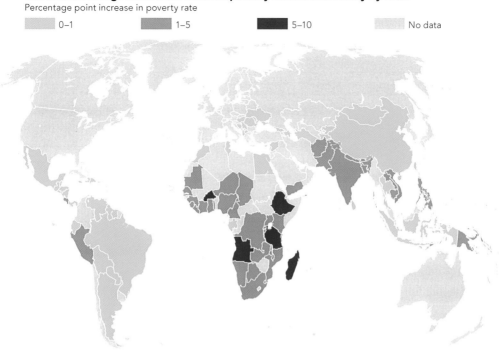

Source: S. Hallegatte, M. Bangalore, L. Bonzanigo, M. Fay, T. Kane, U. Narloch, J. Rozenberg, D. Treguer, and A. Vogt-Schilb, 2016, *Shock Waves: Managing the Impacts of Climate Change on Poverty,* Washington, DC: World Bank, https://openknowledge.worldbank.org/handle/10986/22787.

inevitable; this could have a large impact on poverty reduction efforts.[4] Recent analysis finds that climate change could push more than 100 million more people into poverty by 2030 (figure 13b).[5] But good development—rapid, inclusive, and climate informed—can prevent most of the impacts of climate change on extreme poverty by 2030.

Goal 13 calls for stronger resilience and capacity to adapt to climate-related hazards and natural disasters. Climate change is expected to heighten the intensity of certain natural disasters, such as storms, hurricanes, cyclones, and flooding events. Historically, natural disasters have had a disproportionately adverse effect on low- and middle-income countries, both in

13c Natural disasters have a significant impact on low-income countries and small island developing states (SIDS)
Effects of natural disasters on population and GDP

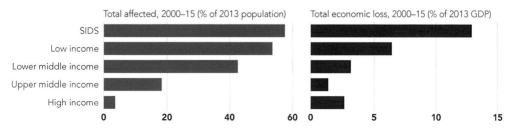

Source: EM-DAT, The International Disaster Database, School of Public Health, Université catholique de Louvain, Brussels, http://www.emdat.be; WDI (SP.POP.TOTL, NY.GDP.MKTP.CD).

13d Climate change is likely to increase global temperatures, with large regional differences

Change in average surface temperature, 1986–2005 to 2080–99 (°C)

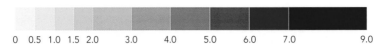

0   0.5 1.0 1.5 2.0   3.0   4.0   5.0   6.0   7.0   9.0

Low emissions scenario, RCP 2.6

High emissions scenario, RCP 8.5

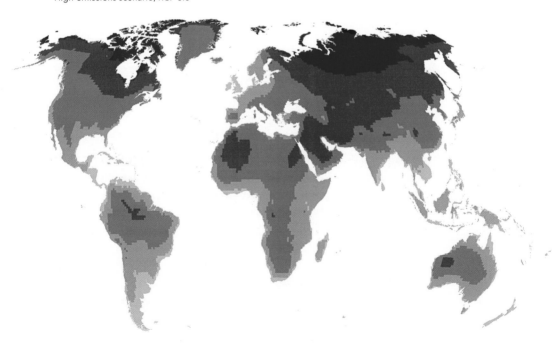

Source: Intergovernmental Panel on Climate Change, 2013, *Climate Change 2013: The Physical Science Basis*, Cambridge, UK: Cambridge University Press; temperature anomaly in 2080–99 using bcc_csm1_1_m model (CMIP5, RCP 2.6 and 8.5). Data are from the World Bank Climate Change Knowledge Portal.

13e Climate change is likely to result in some regions receiving more precipitation while others receive less

Change in average precipitation, 1986–2005 to 2080–99 (%)

-60   -40   -20   -10   0 5 10 15 20   30   40   60   80

Low emissions scenario, RCP 2.6

High emissions scenario, RCP 8.5

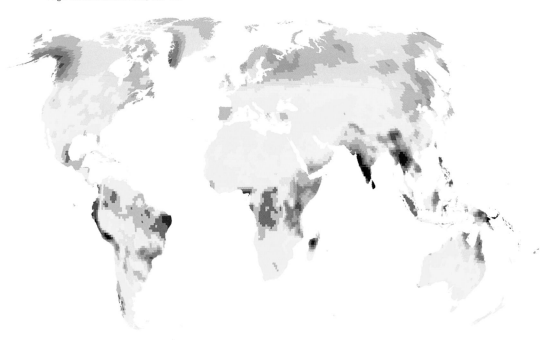

Source: Intergovernmental Panel on Climate Change, 2013, *Climate Change 2013: The Physical Science Basis*, Cambridge, UK: Cambridge University Press; temperature anomaly in 2080–99 using bcc_csm1_1_m model (CMIP5, RCP 2.6 and 8.5). Data are from the World Bank Climate Change Knowledge Portal.

the percentage of population affected and the relative loss of GDP (figure 13c). Small Island Developing States are particularly vulnerable, owing to their exposure to cyclones, their low elevation, and in some cases their economic vulnerability or lack of capacity. Given the expected increase in storm intensity attributable to climate change, these impacts could be even greater in the future.

Addressing climate change

Integrating climate change measures into national policies, strategies, and planning is critical (target 13.2). The December 2015 Paris Agreement under the United Nations Framework Convention on Climate Change (UNFCCC) aims to hold increases in the global average temperature to well below 2° C above preindustrial levels and to reach peak global greenhouse gas emissions as soon as possible with rapid reductions thereafter.

Parties to the UNFCCC have submitted nationally determined contributions (NDCs) detailing intended actions to address climate change. As of November 2016, 162 NDCs have been submitted by 189 countries. NDCs include measures to reduce greenhouse gas emissions (mitigation), better manage climate change impacts on socioeconomic systems and ecosystems (adaptation), and support national policies and planning (both mitigation and adaptation). They cover a wide range of sectors, including energy, agriculture, water, health, and disaster risk management (figure 13f).

Fifty countries' NDCs include cost estimates for implementation totaling US $5.1 trillion. Overall, 112 countries mentioned that they will require financial support for NDC implementation, 108 will require support for technology

13f Nationally determined contributions span many sectors
Number of countries with commitments

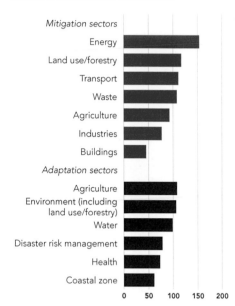

Source: World Bank, Intended Nationally Determined Contributions (http://indc.worldbank.org).

transfer, and 104 will require support for capacity building initiatives.

Financing the response to climate change

The UNFCCC established a goal of committing $100 billion a year by 2020 from developed countries to address the mitigation and adaptation needs of developing countries (target 13.a).[6] In total, the OECD projects climate finance flows attributable to developed countries to be almost $93 billion in 2020, with around $67 billion from public sources, up from $43.5 billion in 2014. Export credits may account for an estimated $1.6 billion. The estimated contribution from private finance varies depending on underlying assumptions

13g Mobilized climate finance could reach $93 billion by 2020
Climate finance ($ billions)

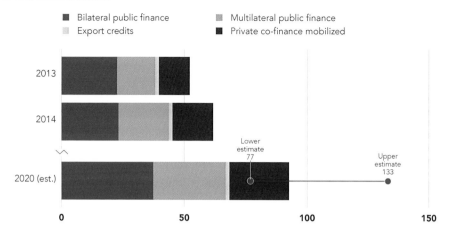

Source: OECD, 2016, *2020 Projections of Climate Finance Towards the USD 100 Billion Goal,* Paris, http://www
.oecd.org/env/cc/oecd-climate-finance-projection.htm.

(figure 13g). Development is moving toward climate-resilient and low emission pathways in many low- and middle-income countries, enhanced by multilateral development bank commitments to increase support for climate change and disaster risk management.

Notes

1. The United Nations Framework Convention on Climate Change is the primary international, intergovernmental forum for negotiating the global response to climate change.

2. Intergovernmental Panel on Climate Change. 2013. *Climate Change 2013: The Physical Science Basis.* Cambridge, UK: Cambridge University Press.

3. Intergovernmental Panel on Climate Change. 2013. *Climate Change 2013: The Physical Science Basis: Summary for Policymakers.* Cambridge, UK: Cambridge University Press.

4. World Bank. 2012. *Turn Down the Heat: Why a 4°C Warmer World Must Be Avoided.* https: //openknowledge.worldbank.org/handle/10986 /11860.

5. World Bank 2016. *Shock Waves: Managing the Impacts of Climate Change on Poverty.* Climate Change and Development. https://openknowledge .worldbank.org/handle/10986/22787. Several approaches are currently being used to estimate the climate finance provided to developing countries. While the multilateral development banks have developed their own agreed methodology, the Organisation for Economic Co-operation and Development approach is presented here because it addresses a wider range of donor sources, and accounts only for contributions from developed countries.

6. United Nations Framework Convention on Climate Change. 2010. "Report of the Conference of the Parties on its fifteenth session." http://unfccc .int/resource/docs/2009/cop15/eng/11a01.pdf.

≋ Life below water

14 Conserve and sustainably use the oceans, seas, and marine resources for sustainable development

Almost 90 percent of global marine fish stocks are now fully exploited or overfished, and wild capture fisheries struggle without sound regulatory frameworks and strong enforcement. The status of marine biodiversity is closely connected with ocean pollution and acidification. About two-thirds of the world's oceans showed signs of increased human impact between 2008 and 2013. Goal 14 recognizes these broad challenges and seeks the conservation and sustainable use of oceans.

Preserving fish stocks for future generations

Driven by rising populations, higher incomes, and greater awareness of seafood's health benefits, the demand for fish is twice the estimated supply of sustainably caught wild fish.[1] Data deficiencies continue to hamper analysis, but aggregates based on data that governments report to the Food and Agriculture Organization (FAO) and estimates of underreporting indicate that total fish catches are declining worldwide (figure 14a).

Goal 14 aims to rapidly rebuild sustainable fish stocks (target 14.4). According to FAO, the proportion of overfished stocks has been increasing over the last four decades.[2]

The situation is worst in low-income and middle-income countries, where weak regulation and enforcement have produced above-average declines. Illegal fishing constitutes an additional challenge, as it accounts for around 20 percent of the global catch, undermining the efforts of both small and large fishing enterprises to implement sustainable fishing regimes and making it harder for well-managed fisheries to compete in international markets by undercutting fair pricing.[3]

14a After decades of growth, fish catches have either plateaued or are declining
Catch (millions of metric tons)

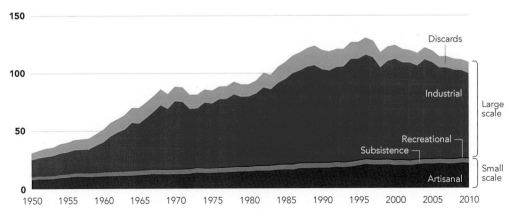

Source: Pauly, D. & Zeller, D. Catch reconstructions reveal that global marine fisheries catches are higher than reported and declining. Nat. Commun. 7:10244 doi: 10.1038/ncomms10244 (2016).

An additional challenge is that global fisheries continue to forgo substantial economic benefits each year due to poor management. And even if the most drastic measures to reduce fishing were implemented globally, it would still take up to 20 years for the overexploited stocks to recover and for global fisheries to be sustainable. The cost of delayed action, compared with accelerated reform, is more than $500 billion.[5]

Eliminating subsidies

Goal 14 supports ocean well-being through the elimination of subsidies that encourage overcapacity and overfishing (target 14.6). Globally, these subsidies, about $10 billion annually and mainly directed to sea fisheries, drive continued fishing despite declining catch values and profits (figures 14b and 14c).[4]

Meeting more demand through aquaculture

As capture fisheries struggle with overcapacity and weak regulatory frameworks, aquaculture has been steadily increasing output to meet rising consumer demand. Aquaculture now provides half the global seafood supply, with China the leading producer (58 percent of total), followed by Indonesia, India, and Vietnam (figure 14e).

Supporting livelihoods

About 61 percent of global gross national product is produced within 100 km of oceans.[6] Goal 14 seeks to increase economic benefits to producers from the sustainable use of marine resources, particularly for producers in small states and lower income economies (target 14.7). About 11 percent of the world's people rely on fisheries and aquaculture as the main source of income, and more than 90 percent of them work in capture fisheries in small enterprises in low- and middle-income countries.[7]

FAO data from 2014 indicate that 56.6 million people were engaged in capture fishing and aquaculture in 2014. Over the last decade employment in the sector decreased, almost

14b Most government subsidies for fisheries go to sea fishing

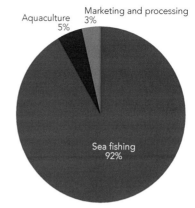

Note: Government support to capture fisheries, aquaculture, and marketing and processing is only for selected OECD countries, but it is indicative of such subsidies worldwide.
Source: Organisation for Economic Co-operation and Development, Fisheries Support (database), Paris, https://data.oecd.org/fish/fisheries-support.htm.

14c Italy and Turkey give the biggest subsidies per catch ton, among OECD countries
Subsidy per metric ton ($)

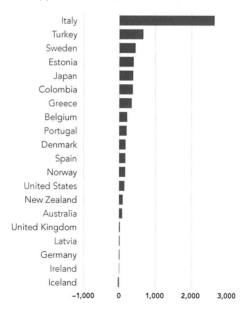

Source: Organisation for Economic Co-operation and Development, Fisheries Support (database), Paris, https://data.oecd.org/fish/fisheries-support.htm; WDI (ER.FSH.CAPT.MT).

entirely due to a decrease of approximately 1.5 million fishers, while the number of fish farmers was stable.[8]

14d Capture fisheries are starting to shrink

Annual catch (per square kilometer)

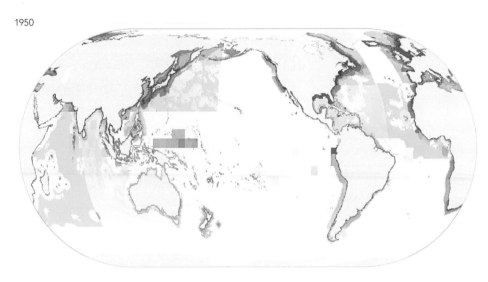

100 g   1 kg   10 kg   100 kg   1 ton   10 tons   100 tons

1950

Change in annual catch (metric tons per square kilometer)

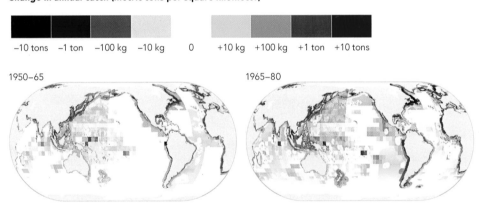

−10 tons   −1 ton   −100 kg   −10 kg   0   +10 kg   +100 kg   +1 ton   +10 tons

1950–65   1965–80

Source: Pauly, D., and D. Zeller, eds., 2015. Sea Around Us Concepts, Design and Data (http://seaaroundus.org)

Capture fisheries production, reported (millions of metric tons)

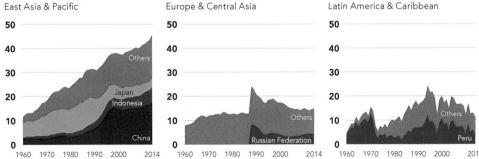

East Asia & Pacific   Europe & Central Asia   Latin America & Caribbean

Source: Food and Agriculture Organization; WDI (ER.FSH.CAPT.MT).

Annual catch (per square kilometer)

100 g   1 kg   10 kg   100 kg   1 ton   10 tons   100 tons

2013

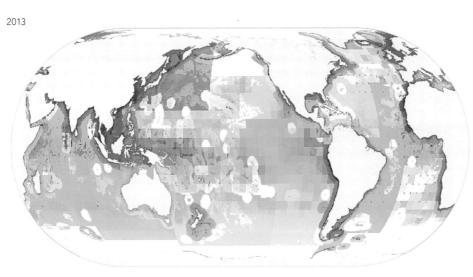

Change in annual catch (metric tons per square kilometer)

−10 tons   −1 ton   −100 kg   −10 kg   0   +10 kg   +100 kg   +1 ton   +10 tons

1980–95   1995–2013

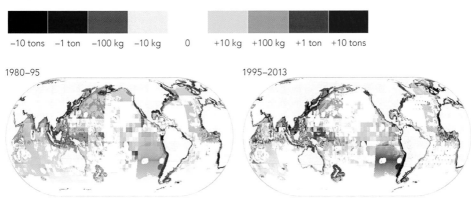

Source: Pauly, D., and D. Zeller, eds., 2015. Sea Around Us Concepts, Design and Data (http://seaaroundus.org)

Capture fisheries production reported (millions of metric tons)

South Asia

North America

Sub-Saharan Africa

Middle East & North Africa

Source: Food and Agriculture Organization; WDI (ER.FSH.CAPT.MT).

14e China is the largest aquaculture producer
Aquaculture production (metric tons)

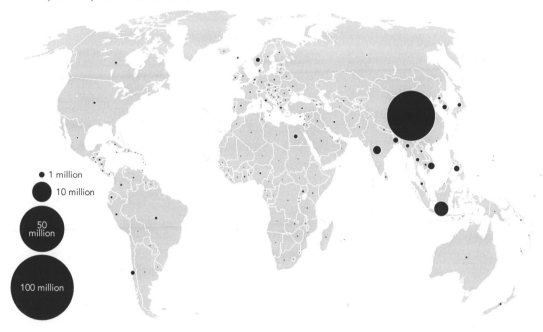

- 1 million
- 10 million
- 50 million
- 100 million

Source: Food and Agriculture Organization; WDI (ER.FSH.AQUA.MT).

Reducing ocean pollution

Marine biodiversity and the global environment are closely connected with ocean pollution and acidification.

Restricting human activities in marine protected areas helps preserve coastal and shoreline ecosystems (target 14.5).[9] If properly enforced, these measures can help rebuild depleted stocks and act as sanctuaries for biodiversity. In 2014 low-income countries had just 3.5 percent of their territorial waters under a protected designation, and high-income countries about 24 percent.

About two-thirds of the ocean area presented evidence of increased human impact in 2013, compared with 2008.[10] The cumulative impact encompasses effects of commercial fishing, climate change, and other ocean and land-based factors. Highly affected areas are places where nearly all pressures converge, as in the North Sea and the South and East China Seas (figure 14f). An overwhelming share of the global ocean (98 percent) is affected by multiple factors, including higher than normal sea surface temperatures, ocean acidification, and high ultraviolet radiation.[11]

Increasing CO_2 concentrations in the atmosphere increase the acidity of the oceans, compromising marine life by making shell formation more difficult. Since the industrial revolution, surface ocean acidity has increased by 30 percent, threatening the multibillion-dollar shellfish industry and the marine ecosystems that depend on clams, oysters, and mussels for water filtration.

Data challenges

Globally, data on fishing and fish stocks are insufficient to support proper management. While stock status is fairly well known in industrialized countries, 80 percent of captures are in countries with little systematic fisheries data collection mechanism, and status is often little more than an educated guess.[12] A concerted national and international effort is needed to collect, analyze, and interpret fishing data for policymaking.

14f Cumulative human impact to marine ecosystems in 2013

Impact score (0, lowest, to 16, highest)

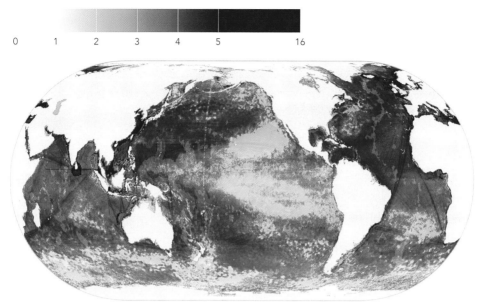

Source: Halpern, B. S. et al. Spatial and temporal changes in cumulative human impacts on the world's ocean. Nat. Commun. 6:7615 doi: 10.1038/ncomms8615 (2015).

Notes

1. Netherlands Environmental Assessment Agency. 2010. *Rethinking Global Biodiversity Strategies: Exploring Structural Changes in Production and Consumption to Reduce Biodiversity Loss*. The Hague, Netherlands.

2. Food and Agriculture Organization. 2016. *The State of World Fisheries and Aquaculture 2016: Contributing to food security and nutrition for all*. Rome.

3. Trends in regional estimates of illegal fishing, averaged over five-year periods from 1980 to 2003. Agnew, D. J., J. Pearce, G. Pramod, T. Peatman, R. Watson, and others. 2009. "Estimating the Worldwide Extent of Illegal Fishing." *PLoS ONE* 4(2): e4570.

4. World Bank. 2009. *The Sunken Billions: The Economic Justification for Fisheries Reform*. Washington, DC.

5. World Bank. 2015. *The Sunken Billions Revisited: Progress and Challenges in Global Marine Fisheries. Preliminary results from the forthcoming World Bank study*. Washington, DC.

6. http://www.worldbank.org/en/topic/environment/brief/oceans.

7. Food and Agriculture Organization. 2014. *The State of World Fisheries and Aquaculture 2014: Opportunities and challenges*. Rome.

8. FAO 2016 (see endnote 2).

9. World Bank. 2012. "Marine Protected Areas Vital to Restoring Biodiversity." Washington, DC.

10. Halpern, B., M. Frazier, J. Potapenko, K. Casey, K. Koenig, C. Longo, J. Lowndes, R. Rockwood, E. Selig, K. Selkoe, and S. Walbridge. 2015. "Spatial and Temporal Changes in Cumulative Human Impacts on the World's Ocean." *Nature Communications* 6: 7615.

11. Brummett, R. 2013. *Growing Aquaculture in Sustainable Ecosystems*. Agriculture and Environmental Services Note, No. 5. Washington, DC: World Bank.

12. Costello, C., D. Ovando, R. Hilborn, S. D. Gaines, O. Deschenes, and S. E. Lester. 2012. "Status and Solutions for the World's Unassessed Fisheries." *Science* 338(6106): 517–20.

🌳 Life on land

15 Protect, restore, and promote sustainable use of terrestrial ecosystems, sustainably manage forests, combat desertification, halt and reverse land degradation, and halt biodiversity loss.

Over the last 25 years Brazil lost around half a million square kilometers of forest—around the same area that China gained. Losses and gains are spread across the globe, but the farther south a country, the more likely it is to have depleted forest land, while more northern countries tend to have gained more forests (figure 15a). Human activity can have a detrimental effect on forests and other parts of the environment, and Goal 15 pledges to reduce or reverse these consequences to provide a more viable ecological platform for sustainable development.

Halting forest loss

Forests cover about one-third of all land worldwide and nearly half of this is within Europe and Central Asia and Latin America and the Caribbean. Crucial to the health of the planet and its diverse species and to the livelihoods of one-fifth of the human population, forests contribute to long-term economic growth, social inclusion, and environmental stability. Goal 15 encourages an increase in both afforestation and reforestation worldwide (target 15.2).

The growing demand for forest products and for agricultural land has contributed to an

15a China gained as much forest area as Brazil lost over the last 25 years
Change in forest area, 1990–2015 (square kilometers)

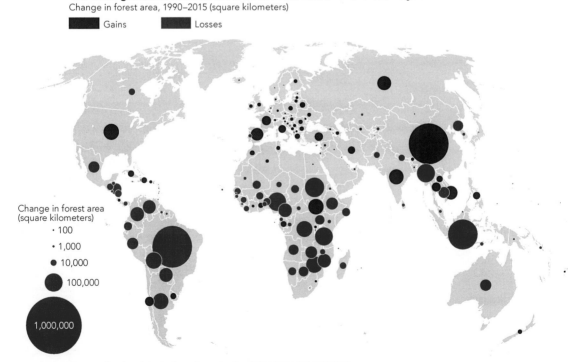

■ Gains   ■ Losses

Change in forest area
(square kilometers)
· 100
· 1,000
● 10,000
● 100,000
● 1,000,000

Source: Food and Agriculture Organization; WDI (AG.LND.FRST.K2).

average annual loss of global forest area of more than 50,000 square kilometers over the last 25 years. This depletion is concentrated in low- and lower-middle-income countries where more than 1.2 million square kilometers of forest disappeared between 1990 and 2015. The biggest losses were in Latin America and the Caribbean, where more than 9 percent of their forest disappeared, and in Sub-Saharan Africa, which had a loss of 12 percent (see figure 15a). High-income economies gained about 191,000 square kilometers of forest land during the last quarter of the century.

Protecting habitats and preserving diversity

Climate change, poaching, overfishing, and pollution come together with the degradation of forests, landscapes, and ecosystems to make the habitat that harbors biodiversity much more vulnerable. Goal 15 seeks to reverse these trends and dampen the threat of extinction to many plant and animal species (target 15.5), especially in Latin America and the Caribbean, Sub-Saharan Africa, and East Asia and Pacific. The number of threatened plants is highest in Ecuador, the number of threatened fish in the United States, the number of threatened mammals in Indonesia, and the number of threatened birds in Brazil (figures 15b–f).

15b Thirteen countries each have more than 500 threatened species of plants, birds, mammals, and fish

Number of species classified by the International Union for Conservation of Nature as endangered, vulnerable, rare, indeterminate, out of danger, or insufficiently known, 2016

	Plants	Birds	Mammals	Fish
Ecuador	1,856	98	45	59
Malaysia	721	50	73	83
Indonesia	427	131	188	158
China	574	89	74	133
Tanzania	602	47	38	176
Madagascar	607	35	120	93
Brazil	521	165	81	86
United States	462	77	35	249
India	388	84	92	222
Mexico	402	61	96	179
Cameroon	490	26	44	119
Peru	326	120	53	50
Colombia	257	119	54	96
Philippines	239	89	39	87
Sri Lanka	291	16	29	54
Vietnam	204	46	55	80
Thailand	150	51	56	106
Kenya	222	39	30	71
New Caledonia	286	16	9	35
Spain	216	15	17	78
Australia	92	50	63	118
Nigeria	197	21	29	71
Panama	208	22	16	54
South Africa	116	46	26	107
Papua New Guinea	152	37	39	56

Source: United Nations Environment Programe; World Conservation Monitoring Centre; International Union for Conservation of Nature: IUCN Red List of Threatened Species; Froese, R., and D. Pauly (eds.), 2008, FishBase database (http://www.fishbase.org); WDI (EN.HPT.THRD.NO, EN.BRD.THRD.NO, EN.MAM.THRD.NO, EN.FSH.THRD.NO).

15c Indonesia and Madagascar have the greatest number of threatened mammal species
Threatened mammal species, 2016

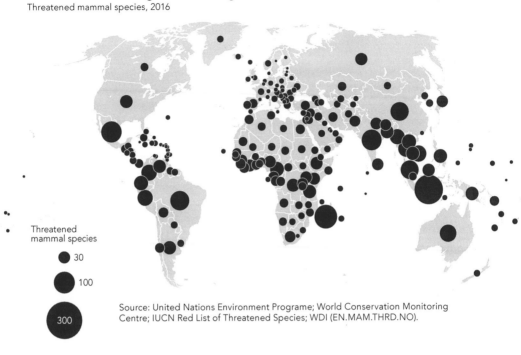

Threatened
mammal species

○ 30

● 100

● 300

Source: United Nations Environment Programe; World Conservation Monitoring Centre; IUCN Red List of Threatened Species; WDI (EN.MAM.THRD.NO).

15d Many species of birds are threatened across Latin America and the Caribbean and East Asia and Pacific
Threatened bird species, 2016

Threatened
bird species

○ 30

● 100

● 300

Source: United Nations Environment Programe; World Conservation Monitoring Centre; IUCN Red List of Threatened Species; WDI (EN.BIR.THRD.NO).

Note: Scales are assigned separately to each map.

15e India, Mexico, and the United States have the largest number of threatened fish species
Threatened fish species, 2016

Threatened
fish species

● 30

● 100

● 300

Source: Froese, R., and D. Pauly (eds.), 2008, FishBase database (http://www.fishbase.org);
WDI (EN.FSH.THRD.NO).

15f Ecuador has substantially more threatened plant species than any other country
Threatened plant species (higher), 2016

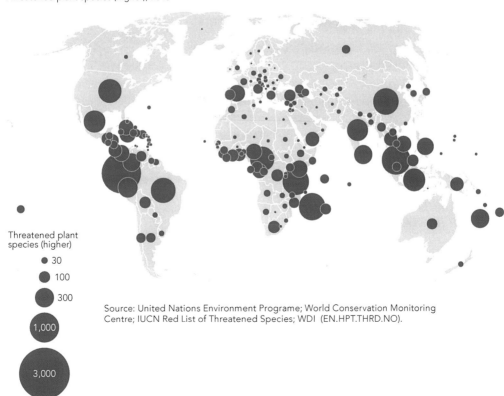

Threatened plant
species (higher)

● 30

● 100

● 300

● 1,000

● 3,000

Source: United Nations Environment Programe; World Conservation Monitoring
Centre; IUCN Red List of Threatened Species; WDI (EN.HPT.THRD.NO).

Protecting land

Worldwide, nearly 15 percent of all terrestrial land is now protected, over 80 percent more than in 1990. Many countries in Latin America protect at least 20 percent of their land, while South Asia lags behind other regions with an average of just under 7 percent (figure 15g).

Restoring forests and degraded landscapes

Restored landscapes support sustainable development in many ways: they benefit livelihoods and biodiversity by reducing erosion, supplying clean water, and providing wildlife habitat, biofuel, and other forest products (targets 15.1 and 15.3). Forests and trees also help mitigate climate change, enhance soil fertility, conserve soil moisture, and boost food production (target 15.3). A restored landscape may accommodate a range of land uses such as agriculture, protected reserves, ecological corridors, regenerated forests, well-managed

plantations, agroforestry systems, and riparian plantings to protect waterways.

Worldwide, nearly 25 million square kilometers offer opportunities for restoration, many in tropical and temperate areas. Nearly 18 million square kilometers would ideally combine forests and trees with other land uses through "mosaic restoration," including smallholder agriculture, agroforestry, and settlements. A further 5 million square kilometers would be suitable for wide-scale restoration of closed forests. Africa provides the largest restoration opportunity, followed by Latin America (figure 15h).

Providing pathways out of poverty

Some 300 to 350 million people, about half of them indigenous, live within or close to dense forests and depend almost entirely on forests for subsistence.[1] And many more in urban areas depend on forest resources for food, energy sources, and construction materials.

15g One in three countries protects at least a fifth of its terrestrial land
Terrestrial protected areas, 2014 (% of total land area)

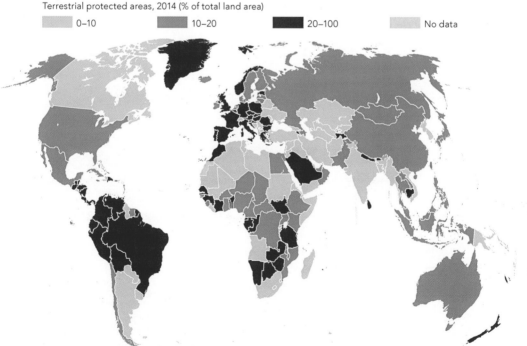

Source: United Nations Environment Programe and the World Conservation Monitoring Centre, as compiled by the World Resources Institute; WDI (ER.LND.PTID.ZS).

15h Africa provides the most opportunities for landscape restoration
Millions of square kilometers

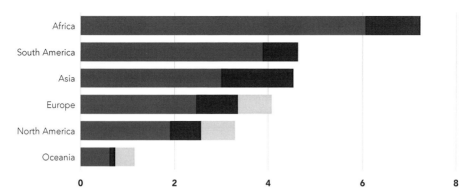

Source: WRI/IUCN, 2011, A World of Opportunity (http://www.forestlandscaperestoration.org/sites/default/files/resource/4._bonn_challenge_world_of_opportunity_brochure_2011-09.pdf).

15i Forest income accounts for around a quarter of all income for rural communities near forests
Sources of income for rural communities with access to forests (%)

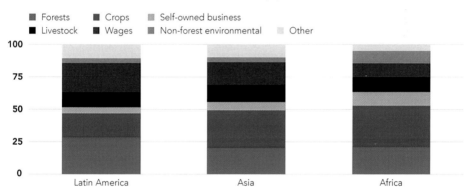

Source: Angelsen, A., P. Jagger, R. Babigumira, B. Belcher, and N. J. Hogarth, 2014, "Environmental Income and Rural Livelihoods: A Global-Comparative Analysis," *World Development* 64(S1).

Beyond subsistence, forests and landscapes are an important aspect of rural livelihoods. Rural households living near forested areas in Africa and Asia derive over 20 percent of their income from forest sources, and those in Latin America derive over 28 percent from forests (figure 15i).[2] About half the income from forests is noncash and includes food, fodder, energy, medicine, and house-building materials. This noncash contribution, or "hidden harvest," is especially important for people living in extreme poverty.

Notes

1. S. Chao. 2012. *Forest Peoples: Numbers Across the World.* Moreton-in-Marsh, UK: Forest Peoples Programme.

2. A. Angelsen, P. Jagger, R. Babigumira, B. Belcher, and N. J. Hogarth. 2014. "Environmental Income and Rural Livelihoods: A Global-Comparative Analysis." *World Development* 64(S1). http://dx.doi.org/10.1016/j.worlddev.2014.03.006. The PEN survey covers about 8,000 households in 24 countries across Sub-Saharan Africa, South and East Asia, and Latin America, and is representative of smallholder-dominated communities living close to forests (with access to forest resources).

Peace, justice, and strong institutions

16 Promote peaceful and inclusive societies for sustainable development, provide access to justice for all, and build effective, accountable, and inclusive institutions at all levels

Nearly one in three firms in countries surveyed in East Asia and Pacific encounter at least one bribe payment request, the most of any region. Businesses in poorer countries are more likely to encounter bribery than those in richer ones, impeding sustainable development. Goal 16 promotes just, transparent, and accountable governance, together with inclusive frameworks and peaceful societies.

Combating bribery in all its forms

Good governance in regulation, business licensing, taxation, and access to public services is fundamental to a sustainable business environment. Opaque, burdensome, and inefficient regulations and procedures nurture opportunities for corrupt officials to extract bribes or unofficial payments, and Goal 16 seeks to minimize these opportunities (target 16.5).

One in four firms in low-income and lower-middle-income countries encounter requests for bribes and informal payments from officials, while one in five are expected to offer gifts to tax officials (figure 16a). Bribery often occurs in transactions necessary for a private firm to conduct business: paying taxes; obtaining an operating license, import license, or construction permit; and obtaining an electrical or water connection.

In the economies worst affected, more than half the firms encounter such requests, adding to their costs (figures 16d and 16e). The requests also impede the creation and growth of firms.

Minimizing violent and conflict-related deaths

The global rate of intentional homicide fell from 6 per 100,000 people to 5 between 2012 and 2014, showing progress toward Goal 16's aim of greatly reducing all forms of violence and conflict-related deaths (target 16.1). Eight countries in Latin America and the Caribbean were in the top 10, with Honduras the most violent at 70 homicides per 100,000 people (figure 16b). In Sub-Saharan Africa, Lesotho had the most homicides at 38 per 100,000 people.

Most battle-related deaths in 2015 were in Syria, at more than 46,500 Afghanistan saw

16a Firms in low- and lower-middle-income countries encounter more bribery than those in other countries

Source: World Bank, Enterprise Surveys; WDI (IC.FRM.BRIB.ZS: IC.TAX.GIFT.ZS: IC.FRM.CORR.ZS).

16b Parts of Latin America and Sub-Saharan Africa had the highest homicide rates in 2014

Intentional homicides, 2014 or most recent year available (per 100,000 people)

0–5   5–9   10 or more   No data

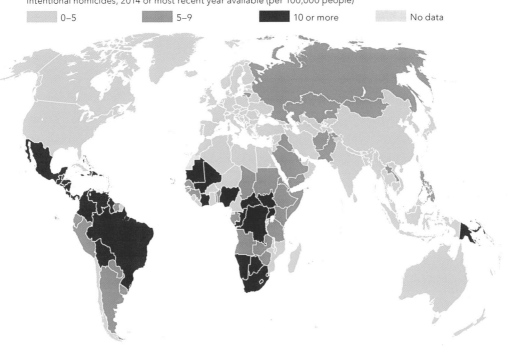

Source: UN Office on Drugs and Crime, Homicide Statistics database; WDI (VC.IHR.PSRC.P5).

battle-related deaths escalate to more than 17,200 in 2015. Conflict casualties rose in Yemen too, with around 6,700 deaths in 2015 (figure 16c).

Achieving good budgetary governance

To provide a sound basis for development, government budgets should be comprehensive, transparent, and realistic (target 16.6). The Public Expenditure and Financial Accountability (PEFA) Program identifies how well governments execute their budgets in accord with the appropriations authorized at the beginning of each year. Since 2005, 147 countries and 178 subnational governments have carried out a PEFA assessment, with national spending more likely to be on target than subnational spending.

Nearly two-thirds of countries surveyed were within 10 percent of their original national budgets, and nearly half of these were within 5 percent. But nearly one in ten countries

16c Syria saw more battle-related deaths in 2015 than any other country

Battle-related deaths in the eight countries with the highest totals in 2015 (thousands)

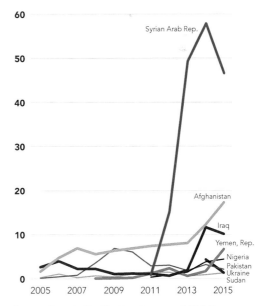

Source: Uppsala Conflict Data Program; WDI (VC. BTL.DETH).

16d Bribery requests are most common in parts of Asia and Africa

Bribery incidence, most recent year available
(% of firms experiencing at least one bribe payment request)

- ■ 30 or more
- ■ 10–30
- ■ 0–10
- ■ No data

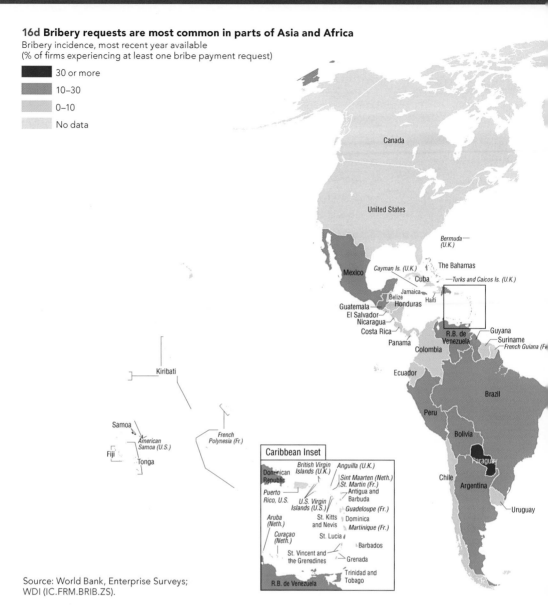

Source: World Bank, Enterprise Surveys;
WDI (IC.FRM.BRIB.ZS).

16e Bribery and informal requests for gifts and payments are common in some countries in Africa and Asia

Top 39 countries where firms experience bribery, most recent year available

■ Bribery incidence (% of firms experiencing at least one bribe payment request)   ■ Firms expected to give gifts in meetings

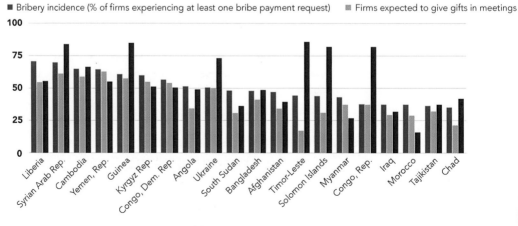

Source: World Bank, Enterprise Surveys; WDI (IC.FRM.BRIB.ZS, IC.TAX.GIFT.ZS, IC.FRM.CORR.ZS).

with tax officials (% of firms)   ■ Informal payments to public officials (% of firms)

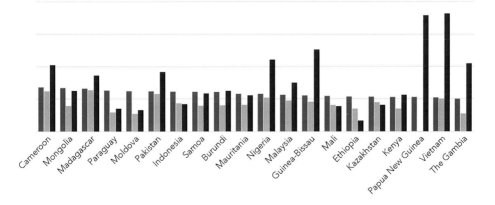

assessed deviated by more than 15 percent. Implementing realistic national budgets is particularly challenging in Sub-Saharan Africa, where nearly four-fifths of countries were more than 5 percent off (figure 16f).

Budget reliability has been assessed at least twice in 102 countries since 2005. Around four of five countries in East Asia and Pacific and South Asia showed improvement, while two of five in Sub-Saharan Africa saw their scores deteriorate (figure 16g).

16f Public spending was within 10 percent of the budget in two-thirds of countries surveyed
Variation from original approved budgets (above or below), most recent year available during 2006–16 (%)

Less than 5   5–10   10–15   15 or more   No data

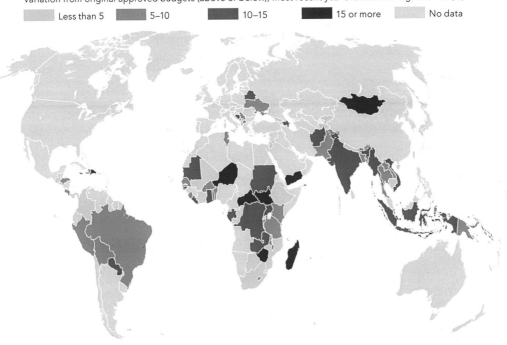

Source: Public Expenditure and Financial Accountability database.

16g More than half the countries with multiple assessments improved budget execution
Change in budget reliability score of countries assessed at more than one time, various years, 2005–16 (percentage of countries)

■ Improved   ■ Deteriorated   ☐ No change

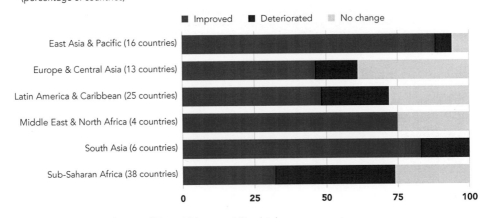

East Asia & Pacific (16 countries)
Europe & Central Asia (13 countries)
Latin America & Caribbean (25 countries)
Middle East & North Africa (4 countries)
South Asia (6 countries)
Sub-Saharan Africa (38 countries)

0   25   50   75   100

Source: Public Expenditure and Financial Accountability database.

Ranging from large states in Brazil to small municipalities in Croatia, almost half the 178 local government budgets surveyed in 34 countries deviated by more than 15 percent from the original budget, and only one in seven subnational budgets was within 5 percentage points (figure 16h). The link between national and subnational performance is not systematic. But Ethiopia and South Africa are good examples of where the majority of subnational and national budgets were very close to the ones the legislature approved.

Bestowing comprehensive legal identity

Civil registration systems should record major life events such as births, marriages, and deaths for all citizens (target 16.9). But in parts of rural Sub-Saharan Africa, birth registration is lacking: in Somalia, fewer than 2 percent of rural births are recorded, and in Malawi and Ethiopia fewer than 5 percent. Civil registration systems are also lacking in some parts of Asia: Yemen and Pakistan record fewer than a quarter of their rural births (figure 16i).

16h Many subnational governments deviated substantially from their planned budgets
Difference between planned and actual subnational budget expenditures, most recent year available during 2006–16

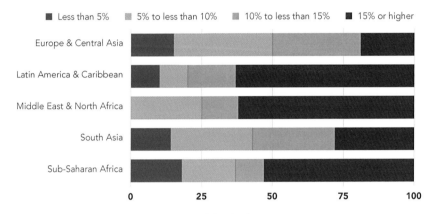

Source: Public Expenditure and Financial Accountability database.

16i In many Asian and African countries, babies in rural areas are less likely to be registered than those in urban areas
Completeness of birth registration, bottom 25 countries for rural registration, most recent value (%)

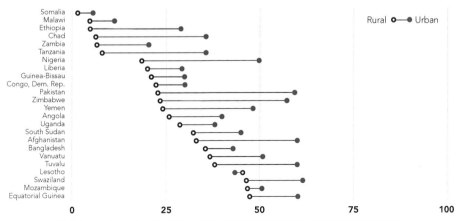

Source: UNICEF, State of the World's Children; WDI (SP.REG.BRTH.RU.ZS, SP.REG.BRTH.UR.ZS).

Partnership for global development

17 Strengthen the means of implementation and revitalize the global partnership for sustainable development

Personal remittances received from across borders and foreign direct investment (FDI) reached $2.7 trillion in 2015, representing 3.6 percent of global GDP. These transfers and official aid enable the poorest countries to lay the foundations for viable long-term development. Funding, capacity building, knowledge sharing, international outreach, debt sustainability, trade facilitation, domestic resource mobilization, effective public–private partnerships, and access to tools and technologies form the basis of Goal 17, which seeks to strengthen global partnerships to support sustainable development.

Rising aid flows

Members of the Development Assistance Committee (DAC) of the Organisation for Economic Co-operation and Development extended $131.6 billion in official development assistance (ODA) in 2015 (figure 17b opposite). After adjustment for inflation and exchange rate valuations, this represents an increase of 6.9 percent in real terms from 2014 and of 83 percent from 2000. But ODA still accounts for a small share of donors' gross national income (GNI), averaging 0.3 percent. Just six DAC countries exceeded the UN benchmark for ODA contributions of at least 0.7 percent of GNI (target 17.2). The three largest donors by volume—the United States, the United Kingdom, and Germany—accounted for more than half of DAC ODA. Bilateral aid to the poorest countries rose 4 percent in real terms in 2015, reflecting the commitment by DAC donors to refocus aid where it is needed most. But much of the increase in flows was attributable to a rise in humanitarian aid rather than to development projects and programs.

Addressing the cost of the refugee crisis

The share of countries' net ODA spent on hosting or processing refugees increased from 5 percent in 2014 to 9 percent in 2015, largely as a result of more refugees arriving in Europe.

In Germany, one of the most affected countries, in-donor country spending on refugees rose to nearly 17 percent of net ODA in 2015, up from 1 percent the previous year. In Sweden the comparable expenditures absorbed nearly 34 percent of net ODA, double that of the year before, and in Austria they accounted for 27 percent in 2015, triple that of 2014. In seven EU countries, in-country spending on refugees was greater than 15 percent of net ODA in 2015 (figure 17a).

17a More aid is being spent in-country on refugee support
Share of aid budgets for in-country cost of refugees (%)

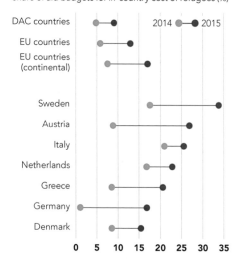

Source: OECD, Development Assistance Committee.

17b Only six countries exceeded the target of providing ODA of at least 0.7 percent of gross national income in 2015

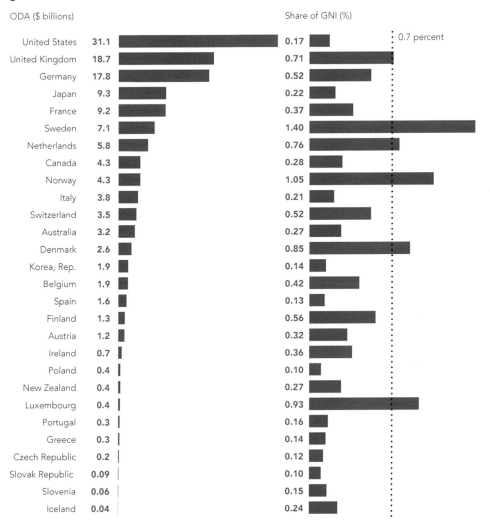

ODA ($ billions)   Share of GNI (%)

Country	ODA	Share of GNI
United States	31.1	0.17
United Kingdom	18.7	0.71
Germany	17.8	0.52
Japan	9.3	0.22
France	9.2	0.37
Sweden	7.1	1.40
Netherlands	5.8	0.76
Canada	4.3	0.28
Norway	4.3	1.05
Italy	3.8	0.21
Switzerland	3.5	0.52
Australia	3.2	0.27
Denmark	2.6	0.85
Korea, Rep.	1.9	0.14
Belgium	1.9	0.42
Spain	1.6	0.13
Finland	1.3	0.56
Austria	1.2	0.32
Ireland	0.7	0.36
Poland	0.4	0.10
New Zealand	0.4	0.27
Luxembourg	0.4	0.93
Portugal	0.3	0.16
Greece	0.3	0.14
Czech Republic	0.2	0.12
Slovak Republic	0.09	0.10
Slovenia	0.06	0.15
Iceland	0.04	0.24

0.7 percent

Source: OECD–DAC.

Increasing foreign direct investment

FDI flows to low- and middle-income countries have increased substantially over the past decade (figures 17c–17e). Such flows are attractive because they are in large part equity investment and thus non–debt creating. They bring such benefits as skills and technology transfer to domestic firms and their labor force as well as productivity gains and greater access to domestic and export markets. Global flows of FDI rose an estimated 22 percent in 2015, to $2.2 trillion, driven by a surge in mergers and acquisitions in high-income countries (figure 17g). FDI proved resilient with the majority of countries posting higher inflows in relation to GDP.

17c FDI flows to low-income countries have been falling since 2011 and stood at around 4 percent of GDP in 2015...

FDI, net inflows to low-income countries (% of GDP)

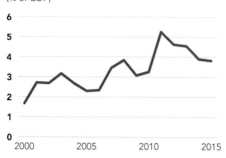

Source: IMF, International Financial Statistics and Balance of Payments databases; World Bank, International Debt Statistics; World Bank and OECD GDP estimates; WDI (BX.KLT.DINV.WD.GD.ZS).

17d ...and in lower-middle-income countries they averaged around 2 percent of GDP in 2015

FDI, net inflows to lower-middle-income countries (% of GDP)

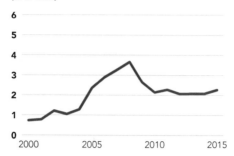

Source: IMF, International Financial Statistics and Balance of Payments databases; World Bank, International Debt Statistics; World Bank and OECD GDP estimates; WDI (BX.KLT.DINV.WD.GD.ZS).

17g FDI net inflows were positive in most countries

FDI, net inflows, 2015 (% of GDP)

- Less than 0
- 0–5
- 5–10
- 10–15
- More than 15
- No data

Source: IMF, International Financial Statistics and Balance of Payments databases; World Bank, International Debt Statistics; World Bank and OECD GDP estimates; WDI (BX.KLT.DINV.WD.GD.ZS).

17e In upper-middle-income countries FDI remained at around 3 percent of GDP...

FDI, net inflows to upper-middle-income countries (% of GDP)

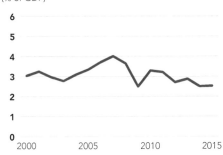

Source: IMF, International Financial Statistics and Balance of Payments databases; World Bank, International Debt Statistics; World Bank and OECD GDP estimates; WDI (BX.KLT.DINV.WD.GD.ZS).

17f ...while in high-income countries it rose from 2 to 3 percent

FDI, net inflows to high-income countries (% of GDP)

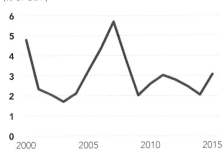

Source: IMF, International Financial Statistics and Balance of Payments databases; World Bank, International Debt Statistics; World Bank and OECD GDP estimates; WDI (BX.KLT.DINV.WD.GD.ZS).

Financing infrastructure through public–private partnerships

Public–private partnerships (PPPs) can make an important contribution to the delivery of efficient public services (target 17.17). Between 1991 and 2015, investments in PPP infrastructure commitments totaled $1.5 trillion in 118 low- and middle-income countries and covered more than 5,000 projects, such as the construction of roads, bridges, light and heavy rail, airports, power plants, and energy and water distribution networks.[1] The average investment in the 65 low- and middle-income countries with investments between 2011 and 2015 was 0.8 percent of GDP. In low-income countries, projects were split equally between the energy and transport sectors, the latter bolstered by a large port terminal in Togo, while in richer countries the energy sector was predominant. Water projects accounted for a negligible investment globally (figures 17h and 17i).

Nearly two-thirds of PPP energy investment in 2015 focused on renewable sources, with solar and wind energy sources accounting for over half (figure 17j).

17h PPP infrastructure investments in low-income countries are split between energy and transport
Average investment in PPP infrastructure projects, 2011–15 (% of GDP)

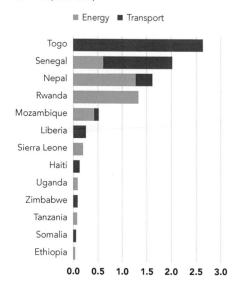

Source: World Bank Private Participation in Infrastructure Database.

17i PPP infrastructure investments in middle-income countries are dominated by energy projects
Average investment in PPP infrastructure projects, 2011–15 (% of GDP)

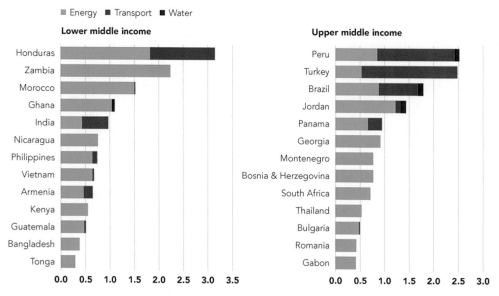

Source: World Bank Private Participation in Infrastructure Database.

17j Investments in wind and solar now account for more than half of PPP investments in energy
Investment in PPP infrastructure projects ($ billions)

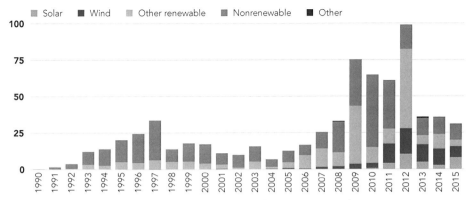

Source: World Bank Private Participation in Infrastructure Database.

Expanding access to the Internet

In 2015 China had the most Internet users of any country: approximately 705 million. Nearly 44 percent of the global population used the Internet (figure 17k), and North America and Europe and Central Asia had the highest rate of users, of fixed broadband subscriptions and of secure Internet servers (target 17.6).

Goal 17 recognizes that enabling the use of information and communications technology in the poorer countries of South Asia and Sub-Saharan Africa will bolster capacity building in science, innovation, and technology. Target 17.8 aims to increase access for people in the 48 Least Developed Countries, where on average, fewer than 13 percent of people have access to the Internet.

17k China has more Internet users than India and the United States combined, but only half its people have access
Individuals using the Internet, 2015 (% of population)

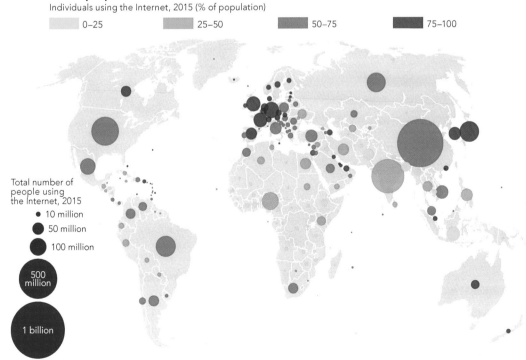

Note: The darker the shade, the greater the share of the population using the Internet. The larger the circle, the more Internet users in a country.
Source: ITU World Telecommunications ICT indicators database; WDI (IT.NET.USER.ZS).

Facilitating trade

Trade is paramount to sustaining development and advancing economic growth, and inclusive trade facilitation is a powerful tool to foster global competitiveness (targets 17.10, 17.11, and 17.12).

Effective and efficient customs processes are fundamental to good trade practices: delays in clearing customs for exports and imports increase costs to firms, interrupt production, interfere with sales, and may result in damaged supplies or merchandise. Clearing customs tends to take longer for imports than exports across most regions, with the longest delays in Sub-Saharan Africa (figures 17l and 17m). Easing the flow of imports into a country helps local manufacturers and businesses obtain component parts of better quality or at lower cost. Enhancing customs capacity to clear exports and imports enables firms to

benefit from a whole spectrum of productivity gains from trade.

In addition to burdensome customs clearance, obtaining necessary documents can be time-consuming and costly for some exports. Within agriculture, cereal exports are subject to more documentation requirements and longer phytosanitary certification than are other product categories, taking on average five days to be processed, compared with just over two days for vegetables. Additionally, the documents necessary to export cash crops tend to be costly (figure 17n).

Traders spend less time on customs clearance in countries with fully operational electronic systems that allow customs declarations to be submitted and processed online. Around 70 percent of countries have fully or partially implemented electronic data interchange systems (figure 17o).

17l Exports take more than 10 days to clear customs in some African and Latin American countries

Days to clear direct exports through customs, most recent year available during 2005–16

| 0–5 | 6–10 | 11 or more | No data |

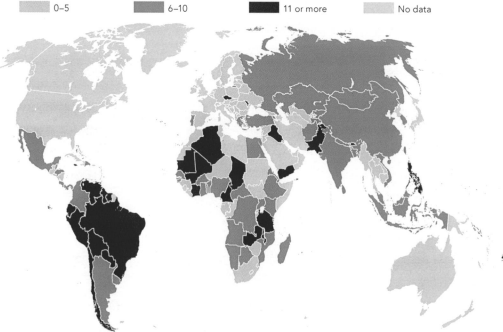

Source: World Bank Enterprise Surveys, http://www.enterprisesurveys.org/data.

17m Imports take more than 10 days to clear customs in many countries

Days to clear imports through customs, most recent year available during 2005–16 (manufacturing firms only)

0–5 ◼ 6–10 ◼ 11 or more No data

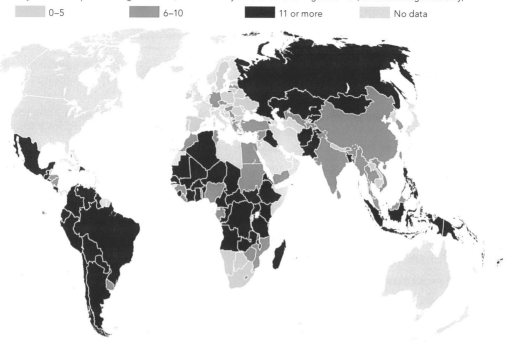

Source: World Bank Enterprise Surveys, http://www.enterprisesurveys.org/data.

17n Obtaining documents is more time consuming for cereal exports than for other agricultural products

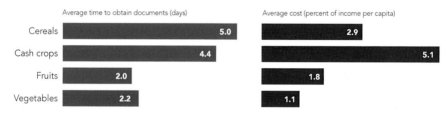

	Average time to obtain documents (days)	Average cost (percent of income per capita)
Cereals	5.0	2.9
Cash crops	4.4	5.1
Fruits	2.0	1.8
Vegetables	2.2	1.1

Note: The sample consists of 40 economies.
Source: World Bank, *Enabling the Business of Agriculture,* http://eba.worldbank.org/.

17o Nearly 70 percent of countries use electronic data interchange systems at the border

Stages of implementation of electronic data interchange systems, 2016 (% of economies)

◼ Fully implemented ◼ Implementation in progress ◼ Not implemented

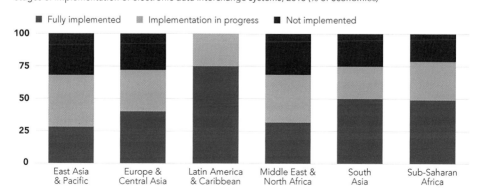

Note: The sample consists of 156 economies.
Source: World Bank Doing Business database.

Building statistical capacity

Timely, relevant, reliable, and high-quality data are fundamental to countries setting their own agendas and to monitoring progress toward national and global development goals. Goal 17 calls on countries to strengthen their statistical capacity by 2020 (target 17.18).

The World Bank's Statistical Capacity Indicator assesses a country's statistical system against numerous criteria on methodology, data sources, and periodicity and timeliness using publicly available information and country inputs. The overall statistical capacity score is then calculated as an average on a scale of 0 to 100.

Since 2004, around two-thirds of countries assessed have improved their scores, indicating a stronger ability to follow internationally recommended statistical methodologies and to collect and disseminate core socioeconomic statistics. But the scores for a third of countries fell between 2004 and 2016. Overall, 26 percent of all countries assessed in 2016 scored over 80, while 16 percent scored less than 50 (figure 17p).

17p In 2016 more than a quarter of low- and middle-income countries scored above 80 on the World Bank's Statistical Capacity Indicator

Statistical capacity score, 2016

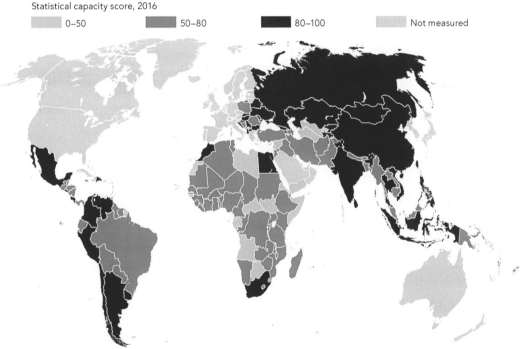

Source: WDI (IQ.SCI.OVRL).

17q Most countries have conducted a recent population census
Census between 2005 and 2015

▨ Conducted a census   ■ Did not conduct a census

Source: United Nations Statistics Division.

A country's score may improve due to a range of factors. For the Dominican Republic more reliable national immunization estimation and a timely agricultural census contributed to an increase in its score from 71 in 2004 to 83 in 2016. For Serbia quality education statistics reported to the United Nations Educational, Scientific and Cultural Organization, use of the Balance of Payments Manual in data compilation, and an agricultural census all helped boost its score from 53 to 90. And for Tanzania improved periodicity of data on child malnutrition and maternal health helped boost its score from 68 to 73.

A population census aims to record the socioeconomic characteristics of the members of each household in a country. Comprehensive surveys are typically carried out every 10 years, but some countries, such as Australia, Canada, Ireland, Japan, and New Zealand, conduct them every five years. Timely censuses, as well as inclusive vital registration systems, are characteristics of a country with high statistical capacity (target 17.19). Only 17 countries worldwide did not conduct a census between 2005 and 2015 (figure 17q).

Notes

1. This figure excludes ICT sector investments because methodological changes for this sector in 2015 render earlier years incomparable.

Sustainable Development Goals and targets

Goal 1 End poverty in all its forms everywhere

1.1 By 2030, eradicate extreme poverty for all people everywhere, currently measured as people living on less than $1.25 a day

1.2 By 2030, reduce at least by half the proportion of men, women and children of all ages living in poverty in all its dimensions according to national definitions

1.3 Implement nationally appropriate social protection systems and measures for all, including floors, and by 2030 achieve substantial coverage of the poor and the vulnerable

1.4 By 2030, ensure that all men and women, in particular the poor and the vulnerable, have equal rights to economic resources, as well as access to basic services, ownership and control over land and other forms of property, inheritance, natural resources, appropriate new technology and financial services, including microfinance

1.5 By 2030, build the resilience of the poor and those in vulnerable situations and reduce their exposure and vulnerability to climate-related extreme events and other economic, social and environmental shocks and disasters

1.a Ensure significant mobilization of resources from a variety of sources, including through enhanced development cooperation, in order to provide adequate and predictable means for developing countries, in particular least developed countries, to implement programmes and policies to end poverty in all its dimensions

1.b Create sound policy frameworks at the national, regional and international levels, based on pro-poor and gender-sensitive development strategies, to support accelerated investment in poverty eradication actions

Goal 2 End hunger, achieve food security and improved nutrition and promote sustainable agriculture

2.1 By 2030, end hunger and ensure access by all people, in particular the poor and people in vulnerable situations, including infants, to safe, nutritious and sufficient food all year round

2.2 By 2030, end all forms of malnutrition, including achieving, by 2025, the internationally agreed targets on stunting and wasting in children under 5 years of age, and address the nutritional needs of adolescent girls, pregnant and lactating women and older persons

2.3 By 2030, double the agricultural productivity and incomes of small-scale food producers, in particular women, indigenous peoples, family farmers, pastoralists and fishers, including through secure and equal access to land, other productive resources and inputs, knowledge, financial services, markets and opportunities for value addition and non-farm employment

2.4 By 2030, ensure sustainable food production systems and implement resilient agricultural practices that increase productivity and production, that help maintain ecosystems, that strengthen capacity for adaptation to climate change, extreme weather, drought, flooding and other disasters and that progressively improve land and soil quality

2.5 By 2020, maintain the genetic diversity of seeds, cultivated plants and farmed and domesticated animals and their related wild species, including through soundly managed and diversified seed and plant banks at the national, regional and international levels, and promote access to and fair and equitable sharing of benefits arising from the utilization of genetic resources and associated traditional knowledge, as internationally agreed

2.a Increase investment, including through enhanced international cooperation, in rural infrastructure, agricultural research and extension services, technology development and plant and livestock gene banks in order to enhance agricultural productive capacity in developing countries, in particular least developed countries

2.b Correct and prevent trade restrictions and distortions in world agricultural markets, including through the parallel elimination of all forms of agricultural export subsidies and all export measures with equivalent effect, in accordance with the mandate of the Doha Development Round

2.c Adopt measures to ensure the proper functioning of food commodity markets and their derivatives and facilitate timely access to market information, including on food reserves, in order to help limit extreme food price volatility

Goal 3 Ensure healthy lives and promote well-being for all at all ages

3.1 By 2030, reduce the global maternal mortality ratio to less than 70 per 100,000 live births

3.2 By 2030, end preventable deaths of newborns and children under 5 years of age, with all countries aiming to reduce neonatal mortality to at least as low as 12 per 1,000 live births and under-5 mortality to at least as low as 25 per 1,000 live births

3.3 By 2030, end the epidemics of AIDS, tuberculosis, malaria and neglected tropical diseases and combat hepatitis, water-borne diseases and other communicable diseases

3.4 By 2030, reduce by one third premature mortality from non-communicable diseases through prevention and treatment and promote mental health and well-being

3.5 Strengthen the prevention and treatment of substance abuse, including narcotic drug abuse and harmful use of alcohol

3.6 By 2020, halve the number of global deaths and injuries from road traffic accidents

3.7 By 2030, ensure universal access to sexual and reproductive health-care services, including for family planning, information and education, and the integration of reproductive health into national strategies and programmes

3.8 Achieve universal health coverage, including financial risk protection, access to quality essential health-care services and access to safe, effective, quality and affordable essential medicines and vaccines for all

3.9 By 2030, substantially reduce the number of deaths and illnesses from hazardous chemicals and air, water and soil pollution and contamination

3.a Strengthen the implementation of the World Health Organization Framework Convention on Tobacco Control in all countries, as appropriate

3.b Support the research and development of vaccines and medicines for the communicable and non-communicable diseases that primarily affect developing countries, provide access to affordable essential medicines and vaccines, in accordance with the Doha Declaration on the TRIPS Agreement and Public Health, which affirms the right of developing countries to use to the full the provisions in the Agreement on Trade-Related Aspects of Intellectual Property Rights regarding flexibilities to protect public health, and, in particular, provide access to medicines for all

3.c Substantially increase health financing and the recruitment, development, training and retention of the health workforce in developing countries, especially in least developed countries and small island developing States

3.d Strengthen the capacity of all countries, in particular developing countries, for early warning, risk reduction and management of national and global health risks

Goal 4 Ensure inclusive and equitable quality education and promote lifelong learning opportunities for all

4.1 By 2030, ensure that all girls and boys complete free, equitable and quality primary and secondary education leading to relevant and effective learning outcomes

4.2 By 2030, ensure that all girls and boys have access to quality early childhood development, care and pre-primary education so that they are ready for primary education

4.3 By 2030, ensure equal access for all women and men to affordable and quality technical, vocational and tertiary education, including university

4.4 By 2030, substantially increase the number of youth and adults who have relevant skills, including technical and vocational skills, for employment, decent jobs and entrepreneurship

4.5 By 2030, eliminate gender disparities in education and ensure equal access to all levels of education and vocational training for the vulnerable, including persons with disabilities, indigenous peoples and children in vulnerable situations

4.6 By 2030, ensure that all youth and a substantial proportion of adults, both men and women, achieve literacy and numeracy

4.7 By 2030, ensure that all learners acquire the knowledge and skills needed to promote sustainable development, including, among others, through education for sustainable development and sustainable lifestyles, human rights, gender equality, promotion of a culture of peace and non-violence, global citizenship and appreciation of cultural diversity and of culture's contribution to sustainable development

4.a Build and upgrade education facilities that are child, disability and gender sensitive and provide safe, non-violent, inclusive and effective learning environments for all

4.b By 2020, substantially expand globally the number of scholarships available to developing countries, in particular least developed countries, small island developing States and African countries, for enrolment in higher education, including vocational training and information and communications technology, technical, engineering and scientific programmes, in developed countries and other developing countries

4.c By 2030, substantially increase the supply of qualified teachers, including through international cooperation for teacher training in developing countries, especially least developed countries and small island developing States

Goal 5 Achieve gender equality and empower all women and girls

5.1 End all forms of discrimination against all women and girls everywhere

5.2 Eliminate all forms of violence against all women and girls in the public and private spheres, including trafficking and sexual and other types of exploitation

5.3 Eliminate all harmful practices, such as child, early and forced marriage and female genital mutilation

5.4 Recognize and value unpaid care and domestic work through the provision of public services, infrastructure and social protection policies and the promotion of shared responsibility within the household and the family as nationally appropriate

5.5 Ensure women's full and effective participation and equal opportunities for leadership at all levels of decision-making in political, economic and public life

5.6 Ensure universal access to sexual and reproductive health and reproductive rights as agreed in accordance with the Programme of Action of the International Conference on Population and Development and the Beijing Platform for Action and the outcome documents of their review conferences

5.a Undertake reforms to give women equal rights to economic resources, as well as access to ownership and control over land and other forms of property, financial services, inheritance and natural resources, in accordance with national laws

5.b Enhance the use of enabling technology, in particular information and communications technology, to promote the empowerment of women

5.c Adopt and strengthen sound policies and enforceable legislation for the promotion of gender equality and the empowerment of all women and girls at all levels

Goal 6 Ensure availability and sustainable management of water and sanitation for all

6.1 By 2030, achieve universal and equitable access to safe and affordable drinking water for all

6.2 By 2030, achieve access to adequate and equitable sanitation and hygiene for all and end open defecation, paying special attention to the needs of women and girls and those in vulnerable situations

6.3 By 2030, improve water quality by reducing pollution, eliminating dumping and minimizing release of hazardous chemicals and materials, halving the proportion of untreated wastewater and substantially increasing recycling and safe reuse globally

6.4 By 2030, substantially increase water-use efficiency across all sectors and ensure sustainable withdrawals and supply of freshwater to address water scarcity and substantially reduce the number of people suffering from water scarcity

6.5 By 2030, implement integrated water resources management at all levels, including through transboundary cooperation as appropriate

6.6 By 2020, protect and restore water-related ecosystems, including mountains, forests, wetlands, rivers, aquifers and lakes

6.a By 2030, expand international cooperation and capacity-building support to developing countries in water- and sanitation-related activities and programmes, including water harvesting, desalination, water efficiency, wastewater treatment, recycling and reuse technologies

6.b Support and strengthen the participation of local communities in improving water and sanitation management

Goal 7 Ensure access to affordable, reliable, sustainable and modern energy for all

7.1 By 2030, ensure universal access to affordable, reliable and modern energy services

7.2 By 2030, increase substantially the share of renewable energy in the global energy mix

7.3 By 2030, double the global rate of improvement in energy efficiency

7.a By 2030, enhance international cooperation to facilitate access to clean energy research and technology, including renewable energy, energy efficiency and advanced and cleaner fossil-fuel technology, and promote investment in energy infrastructure and clean energy technology

7.b By 2030, expand infrastructure and upgrade technology for supplying modern and sustainable energy services for all in developing countries, in particular least developed countries, small island developing States and landlocked developing countries, in accordance with their respective programmes of support

Goal 8 Promote sustained, inclusive and sustainable economic growth, full and productive employment and decent work for all

8.1 Sustain per capita economic growth in accordance with national circumstances and, in particular, at least 7 percent gross domestic product growth per annum in the least developed countries

8.2 Achieve higher levels of economic productivity through diversification, technological upgrading and innovation, including through a focus on high-value added and labour-intensive sectors

8.3 Promote development-oriented policies that support productive activities, decent job creation, entrepreneurship, creativity and innovation, and encourage the formalization and growth of micro-, small- and medium-sized enterprises, including through access to financial services

8.4 Improve progressively, through 2030, global resource efficiency in consumption and production and endeavour to decouple economic growth from environmental degradation, in accordance with the 10-Year Framework of Programmes on Sustainable Consumption and Production, with developed countries taking the lead

8.5 By 2030, achieve full and productive employment and decent work for all women and men, including for young people and persons with disabilities, and equal pay for work of equal value

8.6 By 2020, substantially reduce the proportion of youth not in employment, education or training

8.7 Take immediate and effective measures to eradicate forced labour, end modern slavery and human trafficking and secure the prohibition and elimination of the worst forms of child labour, including recruitment and use of child soldiers, and by 2025 end child labour in all its forms

8.8 Protect labour rights and promote safe and secure working environments for all workers, including migrant workers, in particular women migrants, and those in precarious employment

8.9 By 2030, devise and implement policies to promote sustainable tourism that creates jobs and promotes local culture and products

8.10 Strengthen the capacity of domestic financial institutions to encourage and expand access to banking, insurance and financial services for all

8.a Increase Aid for Trade support for developing countries, in particular least developed countries, including through the Enhanced Integrated Framework for Trade-related Technical Assistance to Least Developed Countries

8.b By 2020, develop and operationalize a global strategy for youth employment and implement the Global Jobs Pact of the International Labour Organization

Goal 9 Build resilient infrastructure, promote inclusive and sustainable industrialization and foster innovation

9.1   Develop quality, reliable, sustainable and resilient infrastructure, including regional and transborder infrastructure, to support economic development and human well-being, with a focus on affordable and equitable access for all

9.2   Promote inclusive and sustainable industrialization and, by 2030, significantly raise industry's share of employment and gross domestic product, in line with national circumstances, and double its share in least developed countries

9.3   Increase the access of small-scale industrial and other enterprises, in particular in developing countries, to financial services, including affordable credit, and their integration into value chains and markets

9.4   By 2030, upgrade infrastructure and retrofit industries to make them sustainable, with increased resource-use efficiency and greater adoption of clean and environmentally sound technologies and industrial processes, with all countries taking action in accordance with their respective capabilities

9.5   Enhance scientific research, upgrade the technological capabilities of industrial sectors in all countries, in particular developing countries, including, by 2030, encouraging innovation and substantially increasing the number of research and development workers per 1 million people and public and private research and development spending

9.a   Facilitate sustainable and resilient infrastructure development in developing countries through enhanced financial, technological and technical support to African countries, least developed countries, landlocked developing countries and small island developing States

9.b   Support domestic technology development, research and innovation in developing countries, including by ensuring a conducive policy environment for, inter alia, industrial diversification and value addition to commodities

9.c   Significantly increase access to information and communications technology and strive to provide universal and affordable access to the Internet in least developed countries by 2020

Goal 10 Reduce inequality within and among countries

10.1   By 2030, progressively achieve and sustain income growth of the bottom 40 percent of the population at a rate higher than the national average

10.2   By 2030, empower and promote the social, economic and political inclusion of all, irrespective of age, sex, disability, race, ethnicity, origin, religion or economic or other status

10.3   Ensure equal opportunity and reduce inequalities of outcome, including by eliminating discriminatory laws, policies and practices and promoting appropriate legislation, policies and action in this regard

10.4   Adopt policies, especially fiscal, wage and social protection policies, and progressively achieve greater equality

10.5   Improve the regulation and monitoring of global financial markets and institutions and strengthen the implementation of such regulations

10.6   Ensure enhanced representation and voice for developing countries in decision-making in global international economic and financial institutions in order to deliver more effective, credible, accountable and legitimate institutions

10.7   Facilitate orderly, safe, regular and responsible migration and mobility of people, including through the implementation of planned and well-managed migration policies

10.a   Implement the principle of special and differential treatment for developing countries, in particular least developed countries, in accordance with World Trade Organization agreements

10.b   Encourage official development assistance and financial flows, including foreign direct investment, to States where the need is greatest, in particular least developed countries, African countries, small island developing States and landlocked developing countries, in accordance with their national plans and programmes

10.c   By 2030, reduce to less than 3 percent the transaction costs of migrant remittances and eliminate remittance corridors with costs higher than 5 percent

Goal 11 Make cities and human settlements inclusive, safe, resilient and sustainable

11.1   By 2030, ensure access for all to adequate, safe and affordable housing and basic services and upgrade slums

11.2   By 2030, provide access to safe, affordable, accessible and sustainable transport systems for all, improving road safety, notably by expanding public transport, with special attention to the needs of those in vulnerable situations, women, children, persons with disabilities and older persons

11.3   By 2030, enhance inclusive and sustainable urbanization and capacity for participatory, integrated and sustainable human settlement planning and management in all countries

11.4   Strengthen efforts to protect and safeguard the world's cultural and natural heritage

11.5   By 2030, significantly reduce the number of deaths and the number of people affected and substantially decrease the direct economic losses relative to global gross domestic product caused by disasters, including water-related disasters, with a focus on protecting the poor and people in vulnerable situations

11.6   By 2030, reduce the adverse per capita environmental impact of cities, including by paying special attention to air quality and municipal and other waste management

11.7   By 2030, provide universal access to safe, inclusive and accessible, green and public spaces, in particular for women and children, older persons and persons with disabilities

11.a   Support positive economic, social and environmental links between urban, peri-urban and rural areas by strengthening national and regional development planning

11.b By 2020, substantially increase the number of cities and human settlements adopting and implementing integrated policies and plans towards inclusion, resource efficiency, mitigation and adaptation to climate change, resilience to disasters, and develop and implement, in line with the Sendai Framework for Disaster Risk Reduction 2015–2030, holistic disaster risk management at all levels

11.c Support least developed countries, including through financial and technical assistance, in building sustainable and resilient buildings utilizing local materials

Goal 12 Ensure sustainable consumption and production patterns

12.1 Implement the 10-Year Framework of Programmes on Sustainable Consumption and Production Patterns, all countries taking action, with developed countries taking the lead, taking into account the development and capabilities of developing countries

12.2 By 2030, achieve the sustainable management and efficient use of natural resources

12.3 By 2030, halve per capita global food waste at the retail and consumer levels and reduce food losses along production and supply chains, including post-harvest losses

12.4 By 2020, achieve the environmentally sound management of chemicals and all wastes throughout their life cycle, in accordance with agreed international frameworks, and significantly reduce their release to air, water and soil in order to minimize their adverse impacts on human health and the environment

12.5 By 2030, substantially reduce waste generation through prevention, reduction, recycling and reuse

12.6 Encourage companies, especially large and trans-national companies, to adopt sustainable practices and to integrate sustainability information into their reporting cycle

12.7 Promote public procurement practices that are sustainable, in accordance with national policies and priorities

12.8 By 2030, ensure that people everywhere have the relevant information and awareness for sustainable development and lifestyles in harmony with nature

12.a Support developing countries to strengthen their scientific and technological capacity to move towards more sustainable patterns of consumption and production

12.b Develop and implement tools to monitor sustainable development impacts for sustainable tourism that creates jobs and promotes local culture and products

12.c Rationalize inefficient fossil-fuel subsidies that encourage wasteful consumption by removing market distortions, in accordance with national circumstances, including by restructuring taxation and phasing out those harmful subsidies, where they exist, to reflect their environmental impacts, taking fully into account the specific needs and conditions of developing countries and minimizing the possible adverse impacts on their development in a manner that protects the poor and the affected communities

Goal 13 Take urgent action to combat climate change and its impacts*

13.1 Strengthen resilience and adaptive capacity to climate-related hazards and natural disasters in all countries

13.2 Integrate climate change measures into national policies, strategies and planning

13.3 Improve education, awareness-raising and human and institutional capacity on climate change mitigation, adaptation, impact reduction and early warning

13.a Implement the commitment undertaken by developed-country parties to the United Nations Framework Convention on Climate Change to a goal of mobilizing jointly $100 billion annually by 2020 from all sources to address the needs of developing countries in the context of meaningful mitigation actions and transparency on implementation and fully operationalize the Green Climate Fund through its capitalization as soon as possible

13.b Promote mechanisms for raising capacity for effective climate change-related planning and management in least developed countries and small island developing States, including focusing on women, youth and local and marginalized communities

Goal 14 Conserve and sustainably use the oceans, seas and marine resources for sustainable development

14.1 By 2025, prevent and significantly reduce marine pollution of all kinds, in particular from land-based activities, including marine debris and nutrient pollution

14.2 By 2020, sustainably manage and protect marine and coastal ecosystems to avoid significant adverse impacts, including by strengthening their resilience, and take action for their restoration in order to achieve healthy and productive oceans

14.3 Minimize and address the impacts of ocean acidification, including through enhanced scientific cooperation at all levels

14.4 By 2020, effectively regulate harvesting and end overfishing, illegal, unreported and unregulated fishing and destructive fishing practices and implement science-based management plans, in order to restore fish stocks in the shortest time feasible, at least to levels that can produce maximum sustainable yield as determined by their biological characteristics

14.5 By 2020, conserve at least 10 percent of coastal and marine areas, consistent with national and international law and based on the best available scientific information

14.6 By 2020, prohibit certain forms of fisheries subsidies which contribute to overcapacity and overfishing, eliminate subsidies that contribute to illegal, unreported and unregulated fishing and refrain from introducing new such subsidies, recognizing that appropriate and effective special and differential treatment for developing and least developed countries should be an integral part of the World Trade Organization fisheries subsidies negotiation

* Acknowledging that the United Nations Framework Convention on Climate Change is the primary international, intergovernmental forum for negotiating the global response to climate change.

14.7 By 2030, increase the economic benefits to small island developing States and least developed countries from the sustainable use of marine resources, including through sustainable management of fisheries, aquaculture and tourism

14.a Increase scientific knowledge, develop research capacity and transfer marine technology, taking into account the Intergovernmental Oceanographic Commission Criteria and Guidelines on the Transfer of Marine Technology, in order to improve ocean health and to enhance the contribution of marine biodiversity to the development of developing countries, in particular small island developing States and least developed countries

14.b Provide access for small-scale artisanal fishers to marine resources and markets

14.c Enhance the conservation and sustainable use of oceans and their resources by implementing international law as reflected in the United Nations Convention on the Law of the Sea, which provides the legal framework for the conservation and sustainable use of oceans and their resources, as recalled in paragraph 158 of "The future we want"

Goal 15 Protect, restore and promote sustainable use of terrestrial ecosystems, sustainably manage forests, combat desertification, and halt and reverse land degradation and halt biodiversity loss

15.1 By 2020, ensure the conservation, restoration and sustainable use of terrestrial and inland freshwater ecosystems and their services, in particular forests, wetlands, mountains and drylands, in line with obligations under international agreements

15.2 By 2020, promote the implementation of sustainable management of all types of forests, halt deforestation, restore degraded forests and substantially increase afforestation and reforestation globally

15.3 By 2030, combat desertification, restore degraded land and soil, including land affected by desertification, drought and floods, and strive to achieve a land degradation-neutral world

15.4 By 2030, ensure the conservation of mountain ecosystems, including their biodiversity, in order to enhance their capacity to provide benefits that are essential for sustainable development

15.5 Take urgent and significant action to reduce the degradation of natural habitats, halt the loss of biodiversity and, by 2020, protect and prevent the extinction of threatened species

15.6 Promote fair and equitable sharing of the benefits arising from the utilization of genetic resources and promote appropriate access to such resources, as internationally agreed

15.7 Take urgent action to end poaching and trafficking of protected species of flora and fauna and address both demand and supply of illegal wildlife products

15.8 By 2020, introduce measures to prevent the introduction and significantly reduce the impact of invasive alien species on land and water ecosystems and control or eradicate the priority species

15.9 By 2020, integrate ecosystem and biodiversity values into national and local planning, development processes, poverty reduction strategies and accounts

15.a Mobilize and significantly increase financial resources from all sources to conserve and sustainably use biodiversity and ecosystems

15.b Mobilize significant resources from all sources and at all levels to finance sustainable forest management and provide adequate incentives to developing countries to advance such management, including for conservation and reforestation

15.c Enhance global support for efforts to combat poaching and trafficking of protected species, including by increasing the capacity of local communities to pursue sustainable livelihood opportunities

Goal 16 Promote peaceful and inclusive societies for sustainable development, provide access to justice for all and build effective, accountable and inclusive institutions at all levels

16.1 Significantly reduce all forms of violence and related death rates everywhere

16.2 End abuse, exploitation, trafficking and all forms of violence against and torture of children

16.3 Promote the rule of law at the national and international levels and ensure equal access to justice for all

16.4 By 2030, significantly reduce illicit financial and arms flows, strengthen the recovery and return of stolen assets and combat all forms of organized crime

16.5 Substantially reduce corruption and bribery in all their forms

16.6 Develop effective, accountable and transparent institutions at all levels

16.7 Ensure responsive, inclusive, participatory and representative decision-making at all levels

16.8 Broaden and strengthen the participation of developing countries in the institutions of global governance

16.9 By 2030, provide legal identity for all, including birth registration

16.10 Ensure public access to information and protect fundamental freedoms, in accordance with national legislation and international agreements

16.a Strengthen relevant national institutions, including through international cooperation, for building capacity at all levels, in particular in developing countries, to prevent violence and combat terrorism and crime

16.b Promote and enforce non-discriminatory laws and policies for sustainable development

Goal 17 Strengthen the means of implementation and revitalize the Global Partnership for Sustainable Development

17.1 Strengthen domestic resource mobilization, including through international support to developing countries, to improve domestic capacity for tax and other revenue collection

17.2 Developed countries to implement fully their official development assistance commitments, including the commitment by many developed countries to achieve the target of 0.7 per cent of gross national income for official development assistance (ODA/GNI) to developing countries and 0.15 to 0.20 per cent of ODA/GNI to least developed countries; ODA providers are encouraged to consider setting a target to provide at least 0.20 per cent of ODA/GNI to least developed countries

17.3 Mobilize additional financial resources for developing countries from multiple sources

17.4 Assist developing countries in attaining long-term debt sustainability through coordinated policies aimed at fostering debt financing, debt relief and debt restructuring, as appropriate, and address the external debt of highly indebted poor countries to reduce debt distress

17.5 Adopt and implement investment promotion regimes for least developed countries

17.6 Enhance North-South, South-South and triangular regional and international cooperation on and access to science, technology and innovation and enhance knowledge-sharing on mutually agreed terms, including through improved coordination among existing mechanisms, in particular at the United Nations level, and through a global technology facilitation mechanism

17.7 Promote the development, transfer, dissemination and diffusion of environmentally sound technologies to developing countries on favourable terms, including on concessional and preferential terms, as mutually agreed

17.8 Fully operationalize the technology bank and science, technology and innovation capacity-building mechanism for least developed countries by 2017 and enhance the use of enabling technology, in particular information and communications technology

17.9 Enhance international support for implementing effective and targeted capacity-building in developing countries to support national plans to implement all the Sustainable Development Goals, including through North-South, South-South and triangular cooperation

17.10 Promote a universal, rules-based, open, non-discriminatory and equitable multilateral trading system under the World Trade Organization, including through the conclusion of negotiations under its Doha Development Agenda

17.11 Significantly increase the exports of developing countries, in particular with a view to doubling the least developed countries' share of global exports by 2020

17.12 Realize timely implementation of duty-free and quota-free market access on a lasting basis for all least developed countries, consistent with World Trade Organization decisions, including by ensuring that preferential rules of origin applicable to imports from least developed countries are transparent and simple, and contribute to facilitating market access

17.13 Enhance global macroeconomic stability, including through policy coordination and policy coherence

17.14 Enhance policy coherence for sustainable development

17.15 Respect each country's policy space and leadership to establish and implement policies for poverty eradication and sustainable development

17.16 Enhance the Global Partnership for Sustainable Development, complemented by multi-stakeholder partnerships that mobilize and share knowledge, expertise, technology and financial resources, to support the achievement of the Sustainable Development Goals in all countries, in particular developing countries

17.17 Encourage and promote effective public, public-private and civil society partnerships, building on the experience and resourcing strategies of partnerships

17.18 By 2020, enhance capacity-building support to developing countries, including for least developed countries and small island developing States, to increase significantly the availability of high-quality, timely and reliable data disaggregated by income, gender, age, race, ethnicity, migratory status, disability, geographic location and other characteristics relevant in national contexts

17.19 By 2030, build on existing initiatives to develop measurements of progress on sustainable development that complement gross domestic product, and support statistical capacity-building in developing countries